ASSESS and Review

Year 5/P6

Paul Harrison

Published in 2002 by:
Nelson Thornes Ltd
Delta Place
27 Bath Road
CHELTENHAM
GL53 7TH
United Kingdom

02 03 04 05 06 / 10 9 8 7 6 5 4 3 2 1

A catalogue record for this book is available from the British Library

ISBN 0 7487 6939 0

Illustrations by Tech-Set Ltd and Barking Dog Art

Page make-up by Tech-Set Ltd

Printed in Great Britain by Ashford Colour Press

Contents

Introduction

The *Assess and Review Year 5/P6* programme

Nelson Thornes Assess and Review Year 5/P6 is a mathematics assessment programme designed for use with children in Year 5 and meeting the assessment requirements of the *Framework for Teaching Mathematics* and the National Curricula for England and Wales. It offers a variety of assessment activities for each of the key objectives for Year 5 together with photocopiable resources and teaching notes. The programme can also be used in conjunction with the *National Guidelines for Scotland 5–14.*

The *Assess and Review Year 5/P6* book

This book provides teachers with a complete resource for assessing children's learning particularly in the medium term. A variety of assessment activities for individuals, pairs and groups are offered for each key objective. These have been carefully chosen for use within a medium term assessment lesson and to allow for as much teacher observation and questioning intervention as possible. For each activity, there are suggestions for probing questions, checkpoints, and possible weaknesses to look out for together with ideas for further remediating experiences. Photocopiable resource sheets for use with activities are provided towards the back of the book. Two written tests, five mental tests and individual and class record sheets are also provided.

The *Assess and Review Year 5/P6* philosophy

Children learn in a variety of ways. To make valid assessments of children's mathematical understanding, they need to be observed engaged in different types of activity such as written, mental and oral activities and games such as those provided in the *Assess and Review Year 5/P6* programme.

Observing children working together at an activity, either in pairs or a group, and listening to their dialogue can give an insight into children's thinking. It is also an efficient means of assessment, making the best use of teacher time. *Assess and Review Year 5/P6* provides a combination of individual, paired and group activities.

Well thought-out, probing questions from the teacher to the child, such as those provided with each activity in *Assess and Review Year 5/P6* are an essential element in assessing the level of children's understanding.

Teachers need to know what to look out for when assessing a child's understanding of a particular mathematical concept. *Assess and Review Year 5/P6* provides some pointers.

National Curricula links

The National Curricula for England and Wales

The activities in this book support assessment for children at Key Stage 2 working within levels 3 to 5 of the National Curriculum for England and Wales. In particular, they support assessment of all of the key objectives of the National Numeracy Framework for Year 5, namely:

- Multiply and divide any positive integer up to 10 000 by 10 or 100 and understand the effect

- Order a given set of positive and negative integers

- Use decimal notation for tenths and hundredths

- Round a number with one or two decimal places to the nearest integer

- Relate fractions to division and to their decimal representations

- Calculate mentally a difference such as $8\,006 - 2\,993$

- Carry out column addition and subtraction of positive integers less than 10 000

- Know by heart all multiplication facts up to 10×10

- Carry out short multiplication and division of a 3-digit by a single-digit integer

- Carry out long multiplication of a 2-digit by a 2-digit integer

- Understand area measured in square centimetres (cm²); understand and use the formula in words 'length $\times$ breadth' for the area of a rectangle

- Recognise parallel and perpendicular lines, and properties of rectangles

- Use all four operations to solve simple word problems involving numbers and quantities, including time, explaining methods and reasoning

The National Curriculum for Wales

The National Curriculum for Wales

The activities in the book will support assessment of most of the teaching of the programmes of study.

This table shows programmes of study and activities in this book that can be used to support their assessment.

Programmes of study	Page	Activity
Understanding number and place value	12	Matching calculations
	12	Real life problems
	13	Dominoes
	14	Ordering tracks
	14	Negative-positive patterns
	15	Temperature changes
	16	One-step targets
	16	Decimal investigation
	17	Biggest wins
	18	Rounding measures
	18	Rounding decimals
	19	Rounding game
	20	Calculator conversions
	20	Finding fractions
	21	Fraction-decimal pairs
Understanding number relationships and methods of calculation	22	Counting up
	22	Target differences
	23	Multiple steps
	23	Calculator steps
	24	Column addition
	24	Column subtraction
	25	Place the digits
	26	Multiplication maze
	26	Speed tables
	27	Criss-cross tables
	27	Multiple towers
	28	Short multiplication
	28	Short division
	29	Biggest and smallest
	30	Long multiplication
	30	Biggest, smallest and nearest
	31	Comparing methods
Solving numerical problems	12	Real life problems
	32	Area problems
	36	Time problems
	36	Practical problems
	37	Mixed problems
Understanding and using properties of shape	34	Feeling shapes
	34	Quadrilateral investigation
	35	Sorting quadrilaterals
Understanding and using measures	32	Areas of rectangles
	32	Area problems
	33	Best estimator

The National Guidelines for Scotland 5–14

The National Guidelines for Scotland 5-14

The activities in the book will support assessment of most of the attainment targets and their strands. This table shows strands and corresponding activities in this book that can be used to support their assessment.

Strand	Page	Activity
Range and type of numbers	12	Matching calculations
	12	Real life problems
	13	Dominoes
	14	Ordering tracks
	14	Negative-positive patterns
	15	Temperature changes
	16	One-step targets
	16	Decimal investigation
	17	Biggest wins
	20	Calculator conversions
	20	Finding fractions
	21	Fraction-decimal pairs
Add and subtract	22	Counting up
	22	Target differences
	23	Multiple steps
	23	Calculator steps
	24	Column addition
	24	Column subtraction
	25	Place the digits
Multiply and divide	26	Multiplication maze
	26	Speed tables
	27	Criss-cross tables
	27	Multiple towers
	28	Short multiplication
	28	Short division
	29	Biggest and smallest
	30	Long multiplication
	30	Biggest, smallest and nearest
	31	Comparing methods
Round numbers	18	Rounding measures
	18	Rounding decimals
	19	Rounding game
Measure and estimate	32	Areas of rectangles
	32	Area problems
	33	Best estimator
Range of shapes	34	Feeling shapes
	34	Quadrilateral investigation
	35	Sorting quadrilaterals
Problem-solving and enquiry	12	Real life problems
	32	Area problems
	36	Time problems
	36	Practical problems
	37	Mixed problems

Using Assess and Review

Short-, medium- and long-term assessment

This book supports short-, medium- and long-term assessment. Activities can be used for different assessment purposes.

Short-term assessment: Specific activities to assess a key objective can be chosen at any time and used for assessment purposes.

Medium-term assessment: During the half-termly assessment week the book can be used to find specific assessment activities which support the key objectives taught during that half term. The results of the tests should be used to inform planning for the next half term.

Long-term assessment: There are end-of-year tests included in the book, both mental tests to read out, with accompanying photocopiable sheets for the children to record their answers, and photocopiable written tests, each of which covers all the key objectives.

Use the assessment record charts on pages 9 to 11 to record the outcomes of your assessments.

Each lesson has sections on:

- **Probing questions:** these are the questions to ask of individuals and small groups to assess the depth of their knowledge and understanding.

- **Checkpoints:** these give specific assessment criteria for the learning objective for that activity. Ask yourself these questions: Can the children do this? Do they know and understand this?

- **Watch for:** these identify what to look for to identify possible misconceptions.

At the end of the set of activities for each key objective there is a table that lists all of the Watch for points and gives suggestions for remediation.

How to use the book

The book is structured as follows:

- activities to support each key objective
- pupil resource sheets containing resources and written activities
- end-of-year written and mental tests.

Planning

For short- and medium-term assessment decide on the key objectives to be assessed, based upon what has been taught during the previous half term. For each key objective taught, plan an assessment lesson. Choose some activities from the book so that one or two groups can be self-supporting in their work, and that you can work with another small group. Prepare resource sheets as necessary. Decide which groups of children will tackle which activity, taking into account the evidence from your existing assessment records. Make a list of the probing questions that you would like to use with your focus group, either as a group or as individuals from within that group. You may want to focus your attention upon those children for whom there is so far insufficient evidence of attainment in the relevant key objective.

Structure of the assessment lesson

Decide whether one of the activities that you have chosen could be used as an oral and mental starter. Explain to the children that they will be working on assessment activities and say which aspect of their learning you intend to assess during that lesson. During the plenary of the lesson return to the probing questions and use these with the whole group to assess a broader range of children's learning. Towards the end of the school year use the mental tests and written tests to assess all of the children. Compare the results of these assessments with your records (see pages 9 to 11) and ensure that the receiving teacher is aware of any forward planning issues for individual children from the results of these assessments.

Resource requirements

In addition to the photocopiable resources provided in this book, you will need the following:

1-6 dice
blank dice
counters
calculators
centimetre rulers
small objects with flat faces
card shapes (including rectangles)
a bag of regular and irregular shape tiles
9-pin geoboards and elastic bands (optional)
a few 2p coins

Links with *Can Do Maths*

Links with *Can Do Maths*: the electronic maths programme

Can Do Maths offers a set of three CD-ROMs for each year in Key Stage 2, providing a worthwhile complement to the *Assess and Review* programme. Each CD-ROM is 'stand alone' and addresses the key objectives within a particular *Numeracy Framework* strand. Between them, the CD-ROMs provide a variety of games, activities and printable resources to add to the range of activities provided in the books. A teacher's section within each CD-ROM contains teacher's notes on each activity, records of children's performances in particular activities and other materials.

Can Do Maths Year 5/P6 links are listed at the end of each section in this book so that it is easy to find the relevant activities. Choose a CD-ROM activity that has the same key objective as the activities selected from this book. This will help the children to focus upon the particular aspect to be assessed. Decide whether to ask children to work individually at the activities or whether they should work in pairs. The CD-ROM activities can be self-supporting, but if possible ask an adult to work with the children using the CD-ROM, so that the probing questions can be asked.

There is further guidance for using the CD-ROM activities in assessment and review lessons and at other times within the *Can Do Maths* teacher's notes.

For more information visit the *Can Do Maths* web site at www.nelsonthornes.com/candomaths or contact the customer services team on 01242 267280.

Class record sheet

Names

Key objectives: Year 5

Objective
Multiply and divide any positive integer up to 10 000 by 10 or 100 and understand the effect
Order a given set of positive and negative integers
Use decimal notation for tenths and hundredths
Round a number with one or two decimal places to the nearest integer
Relate fractions to division and to their decimal representations
Calculate mentally a difference such as 8 006 − 2 993
Carry out column addition and subtraction of two integers less than 10 000
Know by heart all multiplication facts up to 10×10
Carry out short multiplication and division of a 3-digit by a single-digit integer
Carry out long multiplication of a 2-digit by a 2-digit integer
Understand area measured in square centimetres (cm²); understand and use the formula in words 'length × breadth' for the area of a rectangle
Recognise parallel and perpendicular lines and properties of rectangles
Use all four operations to solve simple word problems involving numbers and quantities, including time, explaining methods and reasoning

Tests

Test
Written assessment test 1
Written assessment test 2
Mental mathematics test 1
Mental mathematics test 2
Mental mathematics test 3
Mental mathematics test 4
Mental mathematics test 5

Assess and Review Year 5/P6 © Paul Harrison, Nelson Thornes Ltd 2002

Individual record sheet

Name ....

Key objectives: Year 5	Page	Activity	Comments
Multiply and divide any positive integer up to 10 000 by 10 or 100 and understand the effect	12 12 13	Matching calculations Real life problems Dominoes	
Order a given set of positive and negative integers	14 14 15	Ordering tracks Negative-positive patterns Temperature changes	
Use decimal notation for tenths and hundredths	16 16 17	One-step targets Decimal investigation Biggest wins	
Round a number with one or two decimal places to the nearest integer	18 18 19	Rounding measures Rounding decimals Rounding game	
Relate fractions to division and to their decimal representations	20 20 21	Calculator conversions Finding fractions Fraction-decimal pairs	
Calculate mentally a difference such as 8 006 − 2 993	22 22 23 23	Counting up Target differences Multiple steps Calculator steps	
Carry out column addition and subtraction of two integers less than 10 000	24 24 25	Column addition Column subtraction Place the digits	
Know by heart all multiplication facts up to 10 × 10	26 26 27 27	Multiplication maze Speed tables Criss-cross tables Multiple towers	
Carry out short multiplication and division of a 3-digit by a single-digit integer	28 28 29	Short multiplication Short division Biggest and smallest	
Carry out long multiplication of a 2-digit by a 2-digit integer	30 30 31	Long multiplication Biggest, smallest and nearest Comparing methods	
Understand area measured in square centimetres (cm²); understand and use the formula in words 'length × breadth' for the area of a rectangle	32 32 33	Areas of rectangles Area problems Best estimator	
Recognise parallel and perpendicular lines, and properties of rectangles	34 34 35	Feeling shapes Quadrilateral investigation Sorting quadrilaterals	
Use all four operations to solve simple word problems involving numbers and quantities, including time, explaining methods and reasoning	36 36 37	Time problems Practical problems Mixed problems	

Name ....

Tests	Comments
Written assessment test 1	
Written assessment test 2	
Mental mathematics test 1	
Mental mathematics test 2	
Mental mathematics test 3	
Mental mathematics test 4	
Mental mathematics test 5	

Numbers and the number system

Key objective

Multiply and divide any positive integer up to 10 000 by 10 or 100 and understand the effect

Activity 1 Matching calculations

Learning objective

Multiply and divide any positive integer up to 10 000 by 10 or 100

Organisation

Individuals

Resources

RS1 *Matching calculations*; rulers

Activity

Give each child a copy of RS1 *Matching calculations* and explain what they have to do. Each calculation in the left column has a partner with the same answer in the right column. Children should join the dots next to the partnered calculations with a straight line using a ruler. The lines intersect letters. The children should write each letter, in order, at the foot of the worksheet. Correctly intersected letters, taken from top to bottom, spell WELL DONE.

Extension

Children could make up some pairs of calculations of their own.

Probing questions

- *Can you tell me a quick way of multiplying/dividing a number by 10/by 100? Why does this work?*
- *Why do 6 × 100 and 60 × 10 give the same answer? What about 30 ÷ 10 and 300 ÷ 100?*

Checkpoints

- Can the child quickly find equivalent calculations?
- Does the child understand that when multiplying and dividing by 10 and 100, the non-zero digits remain unchanged and are just shifted to the left or right?

- Has difficulty in quickly multiplying or dividing by 10 or 100
- Lacks understanding of the digit-shifting process involved in adding or removing zeros to or from the end of a number

Activity 2 Real life problems

Learning objective

Multiply and divide any positive integer up to 10 000 by 10 or 100 to solve word problems involving numbers in 'real life'

Organisation

Individuals

Resources

RS2 *Real life problems*

Activity

Give each child a copy of RS2 *Real life problems*. Explain that the purpose of the task is to find out how good they are at quickly solving 'real life' problems that involve multiplication or division by 10 or 100. You could suggest that the children time themselves.

Extension

Children could make up their own set of problems involving multiplication and division by 10 and 100

for others to solve.

Probing questions

- *Can you tell me a quick way of multiplying/dividing a number by 10/by 100? How does this work?*

Checkpoints

- Can the child quickly solve real life word problems involving multiplication and division by 10 and 100?
- Does the child understand the process of shifting digits to the left or right when multiplying or dividing by 10 or 100?

- Has difficulty in quickly multiplying or dividing by 10 or 100
- Lacks understanding of the digit-shifting process involved in adding or removing zeros to or from the end of a number
- Has difficulty in multiplying or dividing by 10 or 100 in real life contexts

Learning objective

Multiply and divide any positive integer by 10 and 100

Organisation

Groups of three or four

Resources

RS3 and RS4 *Dominoes* copied onto card and cut out

Activity

Give each group a set of 24 dominoes from RS3 and RS4 *Dominoes*. These dominoes have a number (answer) on one side and a multiplication or division by 10 or 100 on the other. If necessary, demonstrate how to use the cards to play dominoes, ensuring that joining sides match. If three children are playing they should start with five dominoes each; four each if four children are playing. The remaining dominoes are left face down for players to pick up if they cannot place a domino on their turn. The winner is the first child to place their last domino.

Extension

Children could make their own set of twelve dominoes to play with, ensuring that for each calculation the answer is on another domino.

Probing questions

- *Can you tell me what clues you look for when trying to match multiplications/divisions and answers?*
- *Can you tell me a quick way of multiplying/ dividing a number by 10/by 100? Why does this work?*

Checkpoints

- Can the child quickly match calculations and answers?
- Does the child understand the process of shifting digits to the left or right when multiplying or dividing by 10 or 100?

- Has difficulty in quickly multiplying or dividing by 10 or 100
- Lacks understanding of the digit-shifting process involved in adding or removing zeros to or from the end of a number

Watch for	Further experiences
Has difficulty in quickly multiplying or dividing by 10 or 100	Give more practice with games such as the domino game. Make more use of a calculator to multiply and divide by 10 and 100, predicting answers first.
Lacks understanding of the digit-shifting process involved in adding or removing zeros to or from the end of a number	Provide more work on multiplication and division by 10 and 100 using a place value board and digit cards. Observe and discuss patterns on a calculator when multiplying/dividing by 10/100.
Has difficulty in multiplying or dividing by 10 or 100 in real life contexts	Give more practice with multiplying and dividing by 10 in contexts before progressing to 100. Practise simple conversion of measures or money from one unit to another e.g. centimetres to millimetres; pounds to pence.

CD links

See also *Can Do Maths* Year 5/P6 CD-ROM 1

Positive and negative

Key objective

Order a given set of positive and negative integers

Activity **1** Ordering tracks

Learning objective

Order a given set of positive and negative integers

Organisation

Pairs or small groups

Resources

RS5 *Ordering tracks*; RS6 *Digit cards*; a dice
(marked $+, +, +, -, -, -$)

Activity

Give each child one track from RS5 *Ordering tracks*
and each group three sets of cards cut out of RS6
Digit cards. Explain that the aim of the game is to
have a complete ordered track of numbers from
smallest to largest. The digit cards are shuffled and
piled face down. Children take turns to roll the dice
and turn over the top card. The results provide a
negative or positive integer. If they turn over zero,
the dice roll is ignored. The child writes the integer
in a box on their track and the card is put at the

bottom of the pile. As the children generate
subsequent numbers, they must maintain the order
of numbers from smallest to largest. If an integer
cannot be placed, that turn is lost and play moves
on. The first child with a complete track of thirteen
ordered integers wins.

Probing questions

- *Why did you write the integer in that box?*

- *If the result was zero, where would you write it?*

- *Tell me an integer that goes between these two numbers. Which integer is it closer to?*

Checkpoints

- Can the child order positive and negative integers?

- Orders negative integers in the wrong direction

Activity **2** Negative-positive patterns

Learning objective

Order a given set of positive and negative integers

Organisation

Individuals or pairs

Resources

RS7 *Negative-positive patterns*

Activity

Give each child a copy of RS7 *Negative-positive
patterns*. Explain that the sheet shows incomplete
sequences of positive and negative integers.
Children must identify the pattern in the sequence
and write the missing integers. Ensure that the
children understand what to do. If necessary,
discuss the first pattern with them.

Extension

Children could extend each sequence in either
direction. Suggest that they also replicate each
sequence on their calculator using the constant
function.

Probing questions

- *Can you explain the pattern for me?*

Checkpoints

- Can the child identify and complete the pattern in a sequence of positive and negative integers?

- Orders negative integers in the wrong direction

Activity **3** Temperature changes

Learning objective

Calculate a temperature rise or fall across 0 °C

Organisation

Groups of two to five

Resources

RS8 *Temperature cards*

Activity

Give each group three sets of cards from RS8 *Temperature cards* and explain the rules of the game to them. The temperature cards are shuffled and piled face down. The children take turns to turn over and keep the top card of the pile until they each have two cards. They each work out the difference between their two temperatures. The child with the greatest difference keeps their cards. The rest of the cards are returned to the bottom of the pile. When there are insufficient cards in the pile for a full round of play, the child with the most cards is the winner. If necessary, have a practice run before

they start. Suggest that they draw a positive/ negative number line to help them if necessary.

Probing question

- *What tip would you give to someone trying to find the difference in temperature between −6 °C and 8 °C?*

Checkpoints

- Can the child work out the difference between a negative and a positive temperature?
- Can the child work out the difference between a negative and a positive temperature without using a number line?

- Confuses the negative direction sign with the minus operation sign
- Ignores the negative signs when calculating the difference between two temperatures

Watch for	Further experiences
Orders negative integers in the wrong direction	Provide more number line work with arrowheads at each end of the line to indicate direction. Let children identify the positions of various integers. Highlight the symmetry of the number line about 0.
Confuses the negative direction sign with the minus operation sign	Encourage the use of a superscripted negative sign to help, for example ⁻9. Make sure the sign is read as 'negative' as in 'negative nine' (−9).
Ignores the negative signs when calculating the difference between two temperatures	Give more practice in calculating temperature changes using a thermometer or picture of one.

CD links

See also *Can Do Maths* Year 5/P6 CD-ROM 1

Decimals

Key objective

Use decimal notation for tenths and hundredths

Activity 1 One-step targets

Learning objective

Know what each digit represents in a number with up to two decimal places

Organisation

Individuals

Resources

RS9 *One-step targets*; calculators

Activity

Give each child a copy of the RS9 *One-step targets*. Explain to them how to complete the worksheet by writing in each circle a single operation to change one decimal to another in a single step. They should use a calculator to check. Make sure that they understand what to do, by working through the example at the top of the sheet and others if necessary.

Extension

Children could move from the starting number to the target number in exactly two operations or they could move from the starting number to the next whole number.

Probing questions

- *What if you put a pound sign in front of the starting and target decimals? How many pence have you added/subtracted in the step?*
- *What if the starting and target decimals were metres? How many centimetres have you added/subtracted in the step?*

Checkpoints

- Can the child change one decimal to another with a single operation?
- Does the child know the value of each digit in a decimal with two places?

- Has difficulty in working out what to add or subtract to a decimal to change it to another

Activity 2 Decimal investigation

Learning objectives

Know what each digit represents in a number with up to two decimal places and order a set of numbers with two decimal places

Organisation

Individuals or pairs working cooperatively

Activity

Write the digits 1, 2, 3 and a decimal point on the board. Ask the children to investigate and list all the decimal numbers with one and two places that can be made using these digits. For each number they can use two or three of the digits, but the number must be a decimal number. In other words, the decimal point must always go between two digits. There are eighteen possibilities. When the children have made as many numbers as they can, they order the numbers starting with the smallest.

Extension

The children could write more numbers where two or more of the digits are the same. They could also be asked to use four digits, but keep to two decimal places.

Probing questions

- *What can you tell me about the 1 in each of these numbers?*
- *What is the 1 worth if these are the answers to some money problems in a calculator display?*

Checkpoints

- Can the child tell you the value of the digits in a number with up to two decimal places?
- Can the child order a set of decimal numbers with up to two decimal places?

- Has no strategy when comparing and ordering numbers, for example, not comparing the digits in the higher value places first
- Does not know the value of each digit in a decimal number

Learning objectives

Know what each digit represents in a number with up to two decimal places and order a set of numbers with two decimal places

Organisation

Groups of two to four

Resources

Dice

Activity

Each child draws three sets of digit boxes with decimal points to hold three two-place decimals like this: □·□□ □·□□ □·□□. Children take turns to roll the dice and each child writes the number rolled in one of their boxes. Once written, the digit cannot be moved or removed. After nine throws, the child or children with the largest number collects nine points; the second largest number collects eight points; the third largest number collects seven points; and so on down to the smallest number. The child with the most points wins.

Extension

Children could play the game with three sets of four digit boxes.

Probing questions

- *How do you know that this number is larger than that number?*
- *Which digits do you look at first when comparing two numbers?*
- *Can you tell me about the digit 5 in each of these numbers? What if I put a £ sign in front of each of them? What if they are all lengths given in metres?*

Checkpoints

- Can the child order a set of decimals with two places?
- Can the child tell you the value of each digit in a decimal with two places?

- Has no strategy when comparing numbers, for example, does not compare the digits in the higher value places first
- Does not know the value of each digit in a decimal number

Watch for	Further experiences
Has difficulty in working out what to add or subtract to a decimal to change it to another	Provide further practice in identifying the value of digits in a number, for example the '6' in 1·26 (6 hundredths).
Has no strategy when comparing and ordering numbers, for example, does not compare the digits in the higher value places first	Give more practice at comparing and ordering numbers with, some or all of the digits the same, for example 1·23, 1·25, 1·35, 1·53, 3·25, 3·52.
Does not know the value of each digit in a decimal number	Use digit cards and a place value board or an abacus to represent various numbers.

CD links

See also *Can Do Maths* Year 5/P6 CD-ROM 1

Rounding decimals

Key objective

Round a number with one or two decimal places to the nearest integer

Activity 1 Rounding measures

Learning objective

Round lengths and weights with one decimal place to the nearest unit

Organisation

Individuals

Resources

RS10 *Rounding measures*

Activity

Give each child a copy of RS10 *Rounding measures*. Tell them that it shows the lengths of eight of the longest snakes in the world, and the lengths and weights of eight of the smallest mammals. Explain that they must round each measure to the nearest unit. Point out that lengths are given as a decimal number of centimetres or metres with one decimal place, and weights are given as a decimal number of grams with one decimal place.

Extension

Children could use a ruler to measure small items in the classroom. Encourage them to record each length in centimetres and millimetres, as a decimal number of centimetres, and rounded to the nearest centimetre.

Probing questions

• **What are all the other lengths/weights with one decimal place that would round to, for example, 5 centimetres?**

Checkpoints

• Can the child round to the nearest unit a measure expressed as a decimal with one decimal place?

• Does not know how to round measures with one decimal place to the nearest unit
• Does not know in which direction to round measures with one decimal place ending with 5

Activity 2 Rounding decimals

Learning objective

Round a number with one or two decimal places to the nearest integer

Organisation

Individuals

Resources

RS11 *Rounding decimals*

Activity

Give each child a copy of RS11 *Rounding decimals*. Explain what they have to do. Tell them that there is a central column of ten consecutive integers and at the top of the sheet fourteen decimal numbers. They must round, in their head, each decimal number and write it in one of the boxes next to one of the whole numbers. When all the decimal numbers have been allocated, they must provide in the remaining empty boxes more decimal numbers that will round to the given whole numbers.

Probing questions

• **Why have you rounded 35·2 to 35 and not to 36?**
• **How do you know that 38·95 is nearer to 39 than 38?**
• **What instructions would you give someone for rounding decimals with one place (two places) to the nearest whole number?**

Checkpoints

• Can the child round a number with one decimal place to the nearest integer?
• Can the child round a number with two decimal places to the nearest integer?

• Does not know how to round decimal numbers to the nearest integer
• Does not know in which direction to round one-place decimals ending with 5 or two-place decimals ending with 50

Learning objective

Round a number with one/two decimal place(s) to the nearest integer

Organisation

Groups of two to five

Resources

RS6 *Digit cards*

Activity

Give each child an intact copy of RS6 *Digit cards* and give each group four sets of digit cards from RS6, shuffled and piled face down. Children take turns to turn over the top two cards. They use the digits to make a decimal number with one place and round the decimal to the nearest whole number. They cross that number out on their copy of RS6 *Digit cards*. If the number is already crossed out, play moves on. The cards are placed at the bottom of the pile. The first child to cross out all their numbers is the winner. The game can also be played by drawing the top three cards to make a number with two decimal places.

Probing question

- *What pairs of cards could you turn over that would round to 4?*
- *What sets of three cards could you turn over that would round to 4?*

Checkpoint

- Can the child round a number with one decimal place to the nearest integer?
- Can the child round a number with two decimal places to the nearest integer?

- Does not know how to round decimal numbers to the nearest integer
- Does not know in which direction to round one-place decimals ending with 5 or two-place decimals ending with 50

Watch for	Further experiences
Does not know how to round decimal numbers or measures to the nearest integer or unit	Use a number stick or line with consecutive integers marked at either end and the 'half-way' number marked. Children say in which half of the line a given decimal is located and so to which integer it is nearer. Use a ruler to find whether 6·3 cm is nearer to 6 cm or 7 cm. Practise with money: is £6.78 nearer to £6 or £7?
Does not know in which direction to round one-place decimals ending with 5 or two-place decimals ending with 50	Give children practice in learning the convention of rounding 'half-way' numbers upwards.

CD links

See also *Can Do Maths* Year 5/P6 CD-ROM 1

Fractions

Key objective

Relate fractions to division and to their decimal representations

Activity 1 Calculator conversions

Learning objective

Relate fractions to their decimal representations

Organisation

Individuals

Resources

RS12 *Calculator conversions*; calculators

Activity

Give each child a copy of RS12 *Calculator conversions* and a calculator. Explain that the sheet shows a series of fractions in two tables: Table A contains only tenths and hundredths, while Table B contains a mixture of fractions including quarters and fifths. The children must write the corresponding division, following the example given, predict the result of the division and then check their prediction using a calculator.

Extension

Using a calculator, children could investigate fractional equivalents of various decimals with one place from 0·1 to 0·9. For example, $0 \cdot 2 = \frac{1}{5}, \frac{2}{10}, \frac{3}{15}, \frac{4}{20}, \frac{5}{25}, \frac{6}{30} \cdots \frac{10}{100} \cdots$

Probing questions

- *Can you tell me two fractions that are worth 0·4? How many hundredths are worth 0·4?*

- *How many fractions can you give me that are the same as 0·5? What can you tell me about the numerator and denominator in all fractions that are the same as 0·5?*

Checkpoints

- Can the child relate simple fractions to their decimal equivalents?

- Can the child use a calculator to find the decimal equivalents of fractions?

- Has difficulty in relating fractions other than tenths and hundredths to their decimal equivalents

Activity 2 Finding fractions

Learning objective

Use division to find simple fractions, including tenths and hundredths of numbers and quantities

Organisation

Individuals

Resources

RS13 *Finding fractions*

Activity

Give each child a copy of RS13 *Finding fractions*. Explain that on the sheet they must find fractions of numbers and lengths. Before they begin, give them some oral examples, for example, $\frac{1}{5}$ of 10, $\frac{3}{5}$ of 10, $\frac{1}{6}$ of 12.

Probing question

- *Tell me some fractions of numbers that are equal to 2 (5, 10, 15 etc.) How did you work this out?*

Checkpoint

- Does the child use division (and multiplication) to find simple unit fractions?

- Does not relate fractions to division

- Has difficulty finding non-unit fractions such as $\frac{3}{4}$ and $\frac{7}{10}$

Activity 3 Fraction-decimal pairs

Learning objective

Relate fractions to division and their decimal representations

Organisation

Groups of two to five

Resources

RS14 *Fraction cards*; RS15 *Decimal cards*; calculators

Activity

Give each group a set of fraction cards and decimal cards cut out from RS14 and RS15. All the cards are shuffled and spread out face down in front of the group. Children take turns to turn over two cards. If the cards are equivalent, the child keeps them and has another turn. Explain to the children that equivalent cards could be a matching fraction and a decimal or two fractions. If challenged by other members of the group, children could demonstrate the equivalence of a decimal and a fraction using a calculator. If the cards are not equivalent, the cards are turned back over and play moves on. When all cards have been claimed, the child with the most equivalent pairs wins.

Probing questions

- *Can you tell me two fractions that are the same as 0·2? Are there any other decimals that are both fifths and tenths? How many hundredths are the same as 0·2?*
- *How many different fractions can you give me that are equivalent to 0·5, 0·25?*

Checkpoints

- Can the child quickly match a fraction to its decimal equivalent and vice versa?
- Can the child quickly match equivalent fractions?
- Can the child use a calculator and division to find the decimal equivalent of a fraction?

- Has difficulty in relating fractions other than tenths and hundredths to their decimal equivalents
- Does not understand that the same fraction can have different forms, but still have the same decimal equivalent, for example: $\frac{1}{5} = \frac{2}{10} = \frac{20}{100} = 0·2$

Watch for	Further experiences
Has difficulty in relating fractions other than tenths and hundredths to their decimal equivalents	Play matching games such as pelmanism (pairs) or snap. Use a calculator to convert simple fractions to decimals, predicting the result first.
Does not understand that the same fraction can have different forms, but still have the same decimal equivalent, for example $\frac{1}{5} = \frac{2}{10} = \frac{20}{100} = 0·2$	Practise with fraction 'walls' showing equivalent fractions and decimals, for example a wall showing tenths and fifths. Use the wall to show $0·4 = \frac{4}{10} = \frac{2}{5}$.
Does not relate fractions to division	Use counters to find fractions practically, for example finding $\frac{1}{3}$ of 15 counters involves dividing the counters by 3.
Has difficulty finding non-unit fractions such as $\frac{3}{4}$ or $\frac{7}{10}$	Extend the activities above. Once $\frac{1}{3}$ has been found then $\frac{2}{3}$ can be found. Make sure that the child can read fractions correctly: one third, two thirds.

CD links

See also *Can Do Maths* Year 5/P6 CD-ROM 1

Calculations

Key objective

Calculate mentally a difference such as 8 006 − 2 993

Activity 1 Counting up

Learning objective

Calculate mentally a difference such as 705 − 287

Organisation

Individuals

Resources

RS16 *Counting up*; flip chart and pen

Activity

Give each child a copy of RS16 *Counting up*. Explain that they must find differences in the numbers by counting up from one number to another. As an introduction, you could give the children pairs of 3- or 4-digit numbers to find their differences. For example, 275 and 303 or 7 007 and 3 992. For each answer discuss the various steps that the children took in counting up and illustrate the steps on a blank number line. Remind the children that on RS16, they should show the steps they counted up in and write the answer in the box.

Extension

Children could work out similar differences between a 3-digit and a 4-digit number, for example, 798 and 5 010.

Probing questions

- *Could you have counted up in fewer steps? Show me.*
- *If the difference between two numbers is 2 003 what could the numbers be?*

Checkpoints

- Can the child mentally calculate differences such as 705 − 287 and 8 006 − 2 993 by counting up?
- Can the child show how they counted up on a number line to find a difference?

- Uses inefficient ways of finding differences, for example, counting up in ones instead of tens; initially not counting up to a multiple of 100 or 1 000

Activity 2 Target differences

Learning objective

Calculate mentally the difference between any pair of 3-digit numbers

Organisation

Groups of two to five

Resources

RS6 *Digit cards* or 1–9 cards from a pack of playing cards

Activity

Give each group four sets of cards cut out of RS6 *Digit cards*. The children take turns to be the dealer. The dealer turns over three cards to make a target number, for example, 2 3 9. Then the dealer deals each child six cards. Each child arranges all of their cards to make a subtraction, for example 362 − 128. They then work out the answer to their subtraction. Answers can be challenged, in which case the child challenged must demonstrate how they calculated the answer. The child whose answer is closest to the target scores a point. After an agreed number of rounds, the child with the most points wins.

Extension

Children could play the game with 4-digit numbers using more sets of digit cards.

Probing questions

- *Why did you make those two numbers with your cards?*
- *How did you work out the difference between those two numbers? Talk me through your method.*
- *How will you work out whose difference is closest to the target?*

Checkpoints

- Can the child mentally find the difference between two 3-digit numbers?
- Can the child explain the method they used to find the difference between two 3-digit numbers?

- Uses inefficient ways of finding differences, for example, counting up in ones instead of tens; initially not counting up to a multiple of 100 or 1 000

Activity 3 Multiple steps

Learning objective

Find differences by counting up through the next multiple of 100 or 1 000

Organisation

Individuals

Resources

RS17 *Multiple steps*; calculators

Activity

Give each child a copy of RS17 *Multiple steps*. Explain that the children have to find differences by counting up from the smaller number to the next multiple of 100 or 1 000 and from there to the bigger number. Once the two steps have been found, they are added together to find the total difference. Suggest that the children use a calculator to confirm their results. Before they start, go through the example on the sheet to ensure that they know what to do.

Extension

Children could find the difference between two numbers, setting their own target multiple of 10, 100 or 1 000 to aim for. In the same way, they then record the two steps and add them to obtain the total difference.

Probing questions

- *How did you count up to this multiple?*
- *How did you count from this multiple to the final number?*
- *Could you have counted up in a different way? Show me.*

Checkpoints

- Can the child find the difference between a number and the next multiple of 100 or 1 000?
- Can the child find the difference between a multiple of 100 or 100 and a bigger number?

- Has difficulty in counting up to the next multiple of 100 or 1 000

Activity 4 Calculator steps

Learning objective

Calculate mentally the difference between a number and the next multiple of 10, 100 or 1 000

Organisation

Groups of two to four

Resources

RS6 *Digit cards* or 1–9 cards from a pack of playing cards; calculators

Activity

Give each group four sets of cards cut out from RS6 *Digit cards*. The cards are shuffled and piled face down. Children take turns to turn over the top four cards and arrange the cards to make a 4-digit number. They enter the number in a calculator. The child must then calculate the difference between the entered number and the next multiple of 1 000 by entering addition steps into the calculator. For example, if the number entered is 3 429, the next multiple of a thousand is 4 000. This could be reached by entering +1 +70 +500 giving a difference of 571. After they have each had a turn, the child with the largest difference wins a point. After an agreed number of rounds the child with the most points is the winner. Vary the activity by asking the children to aim for the smallest difference between numbers.

Extension

- *Encourage children to find the difference in exactly two steps.*

Probing questions

- Could you have use fewer steps? Show me.

Checkpoint

- Can the child find the difference between a number and the next multiple of 1 000?

- Has difficulty in counting up to the next multiple of 10, 100 or 1 000

Watch for	Further experiences
Uses inefficient ways of finding differences, for example, counting up in ones instead of tens; initially not counting up to a multiple of 100 or 1 000	Provide more practice in counting from a number to just to the next multiple of 100 or 1 000. Use a calculator. One child enters a 3-digit number, the other must change the display to the next multiple of 100 in one or two steps.
Has difficulty in counting up to the next multiple of 10, 100 or 1 000	Give more practice at finding differences using blank number lines to record steps.

CD links

See also *Can Do Maths* Year 5/P6 CD-ROM 2

Addition and subtraction

Key objective

Carry out column addition and subtraction of two integers less than 10 000

Activity 1 Column addition

Learning objective

Carry out column addition of two integers less than 10 000

Organisation

Individuals or pairs

Resources

RS18 *Column addition*

Activity

Give each child a copy of RS18 *Column addition*. Explain that the children must estimate, then calculate, answers to additions using a column method. Before the children start go through the examples of two methods shown on the sheet. The children could choose one of these methods or use a column method of their own for each calculation. The additions are deliberately presented horizontally, to assess children's ability to position digits in the correct columns. Children could work in pairs, checking and comparing each other's calculations. Observing this will provide additional insight into their understanding of the work.

Extension

Children could use column addition methods to add three 3-digit numbers, two 4-digit numbers and several numbers with different numbers of digits.

Probing questions

- *What tips would you give to someone to help them with column addition?*
- *What could you do to check that this addition is correct?*
- *Can you explain how you did this addition? Talk me through it step by step.*

Checkpoints

- Can the child choose and use accurately an appropriate column method of addition?
- Does the child make reasonable estimates of answers?
- Can the child explain a column method of addition referring to place value and the full value of any digits, for example 'carry one ten to the tens column' rather than merely 'carry one'?

- Uses correctly the 'carrying' method of column addition but with little or no understanding

---

Activity 2 Column subtraction

Learning objective

Carry out column subtraction of two integers less than 10 000

Organisation

Individuals or pairs

Resources

RS19 *Column subtraction*

Activity

Give each child a copy of RS19 *Column subtraction*. Explain that the children must estimate, then calculate, answers to subtractions using a column method. Before they start go through the examples of two methods shown on the sheet. The children

could choose one of these methods or use a column method of their own for each calculation. The subtractions are deliberately presented horizontally to assess children's ability to position digits in the correct columns. Children could work in pairs, checking and comparing each other's calculations. Observing this will provide additional insight into their understanding of the work.

Extension

Children could use column subtraction methods to subtract numbers with different numbers of digits.

Probing questions

- *What tips would you give to someone to help them with column subtraction?*

Activity 2 continued

- *What could you do to check that this subtraction is correct?*
- *Can you explain how you did this subtraction? Talk me through it step by step.*

Checkpoints

- Can the child choose and use accurately an appropriate column method of subtraction?
- Does the child make reasonable estimates of answers?

- Can the child explain the standard short column method of subtraction referring to place value and the full value of any digits, for example 'change one ten to ten units and add it to the units at the top of the units column'?

- Uses correctly the standard short column method of subtraction but with little or no understanding

Activity 3 Place the digits

Learning objective

Carry out column addition and subtraction of two integers less than 10 000

Organisation

Individuals or pairs working cooperatively

Resources

RS20 *Place the digits*; RS6 *Digit cards*

Activity

Give each child or pair a copy of RS20 *Place the digits* and two each of numbers 4, 5, and 6 from RS6 *Digit cards*. Explain that for each calculation on the worksheet, they must add the digits 4, 4, 5, 5, 6 and 6 to the boxes so that calculation is correct. Encourage them to use strategies for deciding which digit to put in a box. For example if a digit in the units answer place is 1, then only 6 and 5 could have produced it. Similarly, if the digit in the tens answers place is a 1 and 1 has been carried, then the two digits added in the tens place must be 6 and 4 or 5 and 5 and so on. Encourage children to use digit cards to help them.

Extension

Children could solve similar puzzles, but for the addition of three 2-digit numbers. They could make up puzzles for each other to solve.

Probing questions

- *How did you work out the digit for this box?*
- *What tips would you give someone who was trying to solve these missing digit calculations?*
- *After you have written all the missing digits, how will you check that the two completed numbers are correct?*

Checkpoints

- Does the child show a thorough understanding of column addition and subtraction?
- Can the child use a range of strategies to work out the missing digits?

- Has great difficulty in solving missing digit puzzles or solely uses 'hit or miss' techniques for finding the missing digits

Watch for	Further experiences
Uses correctly the 'carrying' method of column addition but with little or no understanding	Provide more practice with more informal written methods where the process is more transparent and then use the informal and standard methods alongside each other.
Uses correctly the standard short column method of subtraction but with little or no understanding	Provide more practice with full 'decomposition' methods of subtraction where the process is transparent. Then use this method alongside the short column method.
Has great difficulty in solving missing digit puzzles or solely uses 'hit or miss' techniques for finding the missing digits	Children are probably not ready to use short formal methods of column addition and subtraction. Return to more informal written methods (see above). Try missing digit puzzles involving simple addition and subtraction of 2-digit numbers – initially with no 'carrying' or exchanges involved.

CD links

See also *Can Do Maths* Year 5/P6 CD-ROM 2

Multiplication facts

Key objective

Know by heart all multiplication facts up to 10 × 10

Activity 1 Multiplication maze

Learning objective

Know by heart all multiplication facts from the ×6, ×7, ×8 and ×9 tables

Organisation

Individuals

Resources

RS21 *Multiplication maze*

Activity

Give each child a copy of RS21 *Multiplication maze*. Tell the children that this activity will test how well they know the 6, 7, 8 and 9 times tables. Explain that they begin at the 'start' of the maze, working out the multiplications and following the line with the correct answer to the next multiplication, collecting letters as they go and entering them on the lines at the foot of the sheet to make a message. Point out that the first letter (Y) has already been entered. Make sure that the children understand what to do before they start.

Probing questions

- *If someone has forgotten the 6 (8, 9) times table, what tips would you give them to help work it out?*
- *Can you tell me any links between tables that are useful for working out multiplication facts?*

Checkpoints

- Does the child appear to know by heart the multiplication facts from the ×6, ×7, ×8 and ×9 tables?
- If necessary, can the child quickly derive unknown facts from known facts?

- Lacks confidence with particular tables
- Has difficulty in deriving unknown facts from known facts

Activity 2 Speed tables

Learning objective

Know by heart all multiplication facts up to 10 × 10

Organisation

Individuals or small groups working competitively

Resources

RS22: *Speed tables*

Activity

Give each child a copy of RS22 *Speed tables*. Tell them that this sheet will test how well they know all the tables. Suggest that children time themselves as they fill in the answers, going down each ladder in turn. For a child who knows the tables well it should take them less than four minutes. Alternatively children in a group could work competitively to see who completes the test in the shortest time. They could mark their own answers, agreeing on correct answers and using a calculator or multiplication square to check. Five seconds could be added for

each incorrect answer and the child with the most correct answers in the quickest time is the winner.

Probing questions

- *If someone has forgotten the 6 (8, 9) times table, what tips would you give them to help work it out?*
- *Can you tell me any links between tables that are useful for working out multiplication facts?*

Checkpoints

- Does the child appear to recall quickly all or most facts from the multiplication tables up to 10 × 10?
- If necessary, can the child quickly derive unknown facts from known facts?

- Lacks confidence with particular tables
- Has difficulty in deriving unknown facts from known facts

Activity 3 Criss-cross tables

Learning objective

Know by heart all multiplication facts up to 10 × 10

Organisation

Pairs

Resources

RS23 *Criss-cross tables*; counters in two colours; calculators

Activity

Give each pair a copy of RS23 *Criss-cross tables*, a calculator and counters in two colours. Explain the game on the sheet: the children take turns to enter in the calculator any multiplication from the 2 or 10 times tables. If the answer is on the sheet, they place one of their counters over it. They continue until one of them has four counters in a line, vertically, horizontally or diagonally. Point out that the gameboard contains answers for multiplications from all the tables. The game involves knowing which multiplication will produce a particular answer. Encourage the children to play strategically, that is, as well as aiming to claim a line of four, trying to stop their opponent from doing the same.

Probing questions

- *How many different multiplications can you think of that has, for example, 24 as the answer?*
- *What tips would you give someone for finding multiplications that have, for example, 36 as an answer?*

Checkpoints

- Does the child appear to know by heart all multiplication facts to 10 × 10?
- Can the child quickly and confidently provide a multiplication for a given product?

- Has difficulty in matching multiplications with particular products

Activity 4 Multiple towers

Learning objective

Know by heart all multiplication facts from selected tables

Organisation

Groups of 2 to 5

Resources

RS24 *Multiple towers*; dice; calculators

Activity

Give each group a copy of RS24 *Multiple towers*, two dice and a calculator and explain what they have to do: the children take turns to roll the two dice together and make a 2-digit number with the result. If the number is in the 6, 7 or 8 times table, they write it in the correct column of their grid. Point out that they cannot have the same number twice in the same column but they can have it in different columns. The first child to create three towers of numbers is the winner. Before the children begin, demonstrate by rolling the dice to generate a number and ask the children if the number is a multiple of 6, 7 or 8.

Probing questions

- *How many different multiplications can you think of that has, for example, 24 as the answer?*
- *What tips would you give someone for working out what numbers 36, for example, is a multiple of?*

Checkpoints

- Does the child appear to know by heart multiplication facts from the selected tables?
- Can the child quickly and confidently say what a given number is a multiple of?

- Has difficulty in recognising multiples of particular numbers

Watch for	Further experiences
Lacks confidence with particular tables	Encourage the child to learn by heart the tables in question. Set targets of, say, two lines of a table to be learnt each day. Play games such as pelmanism (pairs) or snap in which multiplications have to be matched with answers.
Has difficulty in deriving unknown facts from known facts	Provide more work on patterns within and between tables, for example deriving ×8 table by doubling ×4 table. Provide work with arrays to reinforce commutative nature of multiplication.
Has difficulty in matching multiplications with particular products Has difficulty in recognising multiples of particular numbers	Play games such as pelmanism (pairs) or snap in which multiplications have to be matched with answers.

CD links

See also *Can Do Maths* Year 5/P6 CD-ROM 2

Short multiplication and division

Key objective

Carry out short multiplication and division of a 3-digit by a single-digit integer

---

Activity 1 Short multiplication

Learning objective

Carry out short multiplication of a 3-digit number by a single-digit integer

Organisation

Individuals or pairs

Resources

RS25 *Short multiplication*

Activity

Give each child a copy of RS25 *Short multiplication*. Explain that they should estimate, then calculate, the answers to the multiplications, selecting one of the two standard methods illustrated. Work through the examples before the children start. On the sheet, multiplications are deliberately presented horizontally to test children's ability to set them out correctly. Children could work in pairs, checking and comparing each other's calculations when they have finished. Observing this will provide additional insight into their understanding.

Extension

Children could carry out multiplication of a decimal with one place by a single-digit integer.

Probing questions

- *Roughly what answer do you expect to get? How did you arrive at that estimate?*
- *Do you expect your answer to be greater or less than your estimate?*
- *Can you explain how you did this multiplication? Talk me through it step by step.*

Checkpoints

- Can the child carry out short multiplication accurately and with confidence?
- Does the child understand the processes involved in short multiplication, such as 'carrying'?
- Can the child make reasonable estimates of answers?

- Uses correctly a standard short method of multiplication but without understanding
- Has difficulty in calculating the answers
- Does not know by heart facts from the multiplication tables

---

Activity 2 Short division

Learning objective

Carry out short division of a 3-digit number by a single-digit integer

Organisation

Individuals or pairs

Resources

RS26 *Short division*

Activity

Give each child a copy of RS26 *Short division*. Explain that the children should estimate, then calculate, the answers to the divisions, selecting one of the two standard methods illustrated. Work through the examples before the children start. On the sheet, divisions are deliberately presented horizontally to test children's ability to set them out correctly. Children could work in pairs, checking and comparing each other's calculations when they have finished. Observing this will provide additional insight into their understanding.

Probing questions

- *Roughly what answer do you expect to get? How did you arrive at that estimate?*
- *Do you expect your answer to be greater or less than your estimate?*
- *Do you think there will be a remainder? Why?*
- *Can you explain how you did this division? Talk me through it step by step.*

Checkpoints

- Can the child carry out short division accurately and with confidence?
- Does the child understand the processes involved in short multiplication, such as subtraction?
- Can the child make reasonable estimates of answers?

- Uses correctly a standard short method of division but without understanding
- Cannot derive division facts from the multiplication tables
- Has difficulty in calculating the answers

Activity 3 Biggest and smallest

Learning objectives

Use a standard method of dividing or multiplying a 3-digit number by a single-digit integer and estimate the answer

Organisation

Groups of two to four

Resources

RS6 *Digit cards* or 1–9 cards taken from a pack of playing cards

Activity

Give each group two or more sets of 1–9 cards from RS6 or from a pack of playing cards. The cards are shuffled and placed face down in a pile. Children take turns to turn over the top four cards and use the digits to write a HTU by U multiplication and division in standard format. For example, if 1, 2, 4 and 8 were drawn they could write the following calculations:

$$4\,1\,2 \qquad 4\overline{)128}$$
$$\times 8$$

When all the children have had their turn, they work out their answers. The child with the largest product wins a point as does the child with the smallest quotient. They continue until a child with five or more points wins the game.

Variations:
- the child with the smallest product and the largest quotient win a point
- the child with a division with no remainder wins a point.

Extension

The child could draw five cards and create 4-digit by 1-digit multiplications and divisions.

Probing questions

- *What tips would you give to someone for using their digits to make the largest/smallest answer to a multiplication/division?*
- *Roughly what answer do you expect to get? How did you arrive at that?*
- *How did you work out the answer to that? Show me step by step.*

Checkpoints

- Does the child use a strategy to produce the largest or smallest answer?
- Can the child give an approximate answer to a multiplication or division?
- Can the child carry out short multiplication and division accurately and with confidence?

- Has difficulty in approximating answers
- Has difficulty in calculating the answers

Watch for	Further experiences
Uses correctly a standard short method of multiplication but without understanding. Has difficulty in calculating the answers	Provide more practice with informal written methods, such as the grid method where numbers are expanded and the process is transparent. Start with multiplication of a 2-digit number by a single-digit, explaining the process step by step.
Does not know by heart facts from the multiplication tables	Find out in which tables the child is weak. Set targets of, say, two lines of a table to be learnt each day. Use games such as pelmanism (pairs) or snap in which multiplications have to be matched with answers.
Uses correctly a standard short method of division but without understanding. Has difficulty in calculating the answers	Provide more practice with informal written methods, such as subtracting multiples of the divisor starting with the division of 2-digit numbers.
Cannot derive division facts from the multiplication tables	Use arrays to produce related multiplication and division facts to reinforce the relationship between multiplication and division.
Has difficulty in approximating answers	Give more practice at approximating by rounding numbers to be multiplied to the nearest 100 and then multiplying.

CD links

See also *Can Do Maths* Year 5/P6 CD-ROM 2

Long multiplication

Key objective

Carry out long multiplication of a 2-digit by a 2-digit integer

---

Activity 1 Long multiplication

Learning objective

Carry out long multiplication of a 2-digit by a 2-digit integer

Organisation

Individuals or pairs

Resources

RS27 *Long multiplication*

Activity

Give each child a copy of RS27 *Long multiplication*. Explain that they must estimate and then complete the multiplications in standard long multiplication format. Before they start go through the example at the top of the sheet. Point out that you are looking for clear setting out and accuracy. If children work in pairs, they could check and compare each other's answers when they have finished. Observing this will give additional insight into their understanding.

Probing questions

- *How did you work out the answer to this? Talk me through what you did step by step.*
- *What do you think the answer to this will be roughly?*
- *Show the child some long multiplications with mistakes in them. Ask the child to identify the mistakes and talk through what is wrong.*

Checkpoints

- Can the child carry out long multiplication accurately and with confidence?
- Does the child understand the processes involved in long multiplication such as decomposing the multiplier into its tens and units components?
- Can the child make reasonable estimates of answers?

- Uses correctly the standard method of long multiplication but without understanding
- Does not know multiplication facts by heart
- Has difficulty in multiplying multiples of 10

Activity 2 Biggest, smallest and nearest

Learning objective

Carry out long multiplication of a 2-digit by a 2-digit integer

Organisation

Individuals or pairs working cooperatively

Resources

RS6 *Digit cards* (optional)

Activity

Children choose four digits from 2, 3, 4, 5 and 6 to make:
- the largest product that they can
- the smallest product that they can
- the product nearest to 2 000
- the product nearest to 3 000.

They may find it helpful to have the digit cards from RS6 *Digit cards* to manipulate. For each product they must write the multiplication in standard long multiplication format. When the children have finished, discuss the various approaches they took and the answers they obtained.

Probing questions

- *Which 2-digit numbers would definitely not give the biggest/smallest product? How do you know?*
- *How did you set about finding which 2-digit numbers might have a product nearest to 2 000/3 000?*

Checkpoints

- Can the child estimate the product of two 2-digit numbers?
- Can the child set out a long multiplication correctly?
- Can the child carry out long multiplication accurately and with confidence?

Activity 2 continued

- Does the child understand the processes involved in long multiplication such as decomposing the multiplier into its tens and units components?

- Has difficulty in estimating answers
- Uses correctly the standard method of long multiplication but without understanding
- Does not know multiplication facts by heart
- Has difficulty in multiplying multiples of 10

Activity 3 Comparing methods

Learning objectives

Carry out long multiplication of a 2-digit by a 2-digit integer using informal pencil and paper methods to support, record or explain multiplications

Organisation

Pairs

Resources

RS28 *Comparing methods*

Activity

Cut copies of RS28 *Comparing methods* in half and give each child in each pair either the top or bottom half. Remind the children of the two methods of multiplication used on the sheet. Point out that the multiplications in each half of the page are the same. The children do the first multiplication each using a different method. When they have both finished, they compare answers and methods and identify the corresponding elements in each method. They swap sheets and deal with the second calculation in a similar way, and so on until all four calculations have been completed.

Probing questions

- ***Can you explain to me how the grid/standard method works? Take me through it step by step.***
- ***In what ways is the grid method of long multiplication the same as the standard method?***
- ***Which two numbers is this the product of?***
- ***Where can I find this part of multiplication in the grid method?***

Checkpoints

- Can the child carry out both the grid method and the standard method of long multiplication?
- Can the child explain the processes involved in both the grid method and the standard method of multiplication?

- Uses correctly the standard method of long multiplication but without understanding
- Does not know multiplication facts by heart
- Has difficulty in multiplying multiples of 10

Watch for	Further experiences
Uses correctly the standard method of long multiplication but without understanding	Use a grid method alongside the long multiplication method and compare and discuss the various elements and sub-products in each method.
Does not know the multiplication facts by heart	Ascertain which tables the child is unsure about and then set targets for learning them, for example, learning two facts from the table each day. Use games such as pelmanism (pairs) in which the child has to match answers to multiplications.
Has difficulty in multiplying multiples of 10	Revise multiplication by 10. Use a calculator to show that, for example, 32×40 is ten times bigger than 32×4, that is $32 \times 40 = 32 \times 4 \times 10$.
Has difficulty in estimating answers	Demonstrate how to round each number to the nearest 10 and then multiply to obtain an approximate answer, for example 29×34 is approximately $30 \times 30 = 900$. Encourage them always to estimate an answer before carrying out a calculation.

CD links

See also *Can Do Maths* Year 5/P6 CD-ROM 2

Measures

Key objective

Understand area measured in square centimetres (cm²); understand and use the formula in words 'length × breadth' for the area of a rectangle

---

Activity 1 Areas of rectangles

Learning objectives

Understand area measured in square centimetres (cm²) and understand and use the formula in words 'length × breadth' for the area of a rectangle

Organisation

Individuals

Resources

RS29 *Areas of rectangles*; RS30 *Grid of centimetre squares* (for Extension)

Activity

Give each child a copy of RS29 *Areas of rectangles* and explain that they must find the areas of rectangles on a grid of centimetre squares. As the rectangles are opaque, children will not be able to find the areas by counting squares. Before they begin ensure that they know how to find the area of a rectangle and point out that they will need either to apply the formula for the area of a rectangle directly or use it indirectly by working out the number of centimetre squares in a row, the number of rows and multiplying.

Extension

Using RS30 *Grid of centimetre squares*, children could investigate which rectangle with a perimeter of 24 cm has the largest area.

Probing questions

- *How did you find the area of this rectangle? Talk me through what you did.*
- *Is there a quicker way of finding the area?*
- *What would happen to the area if the length/width of this rectangle was increased by a centimetre?*

Checkpoints

- Does the child show understanding when finding the areas of shapes?
- Does the child use the formula when finding the areas of rectangles?

- Counts imaginary centimetre squares one by one

Activity 2 Area problems

Learning objectives

Understand and use the formula for the area of a rectangle to solve 'real life' problems.

Organisation

Individuals

Resources

RS31 *Area problems*

Activity

Give each child a copy of RS31 *Area problems*. Explain that they must use their understanding of the area of rectangles to solve 'real life' problems. Point out that question 5 is an investigation and not a straightforward calculation.

Probing question

- *How did you work out the answer to that? Talk me through what you did step by step.*

Checkpoints

- Does the child show an understanding of area when solving 'real life' problems?
- Does the child show an understanding of the formula for the area of rectangles when solving 'real life' problems?

- Does not know or use the formula for the area of rectangles
- Has poor understanding of area in terms of square units

Activity 3 Best estimator

Learning objectives

Understand area measured in square centimetres (cm^2) and understand and use the formula in words 'length $\times$ breadth' for the area of a rectangle

Organisation

Groups of two to four children in competition or individuals

Resources

RS32 *Best estimator*; centimetre rulers

Activity

Give each child a copy of RS32 *Best estimator* and explain that they must estimate the area of each rectangle and write the estimated area. They then measure the length and breadth of each rectangle, calculate the area, and write the actual area. Then they work out the difference between the estimated area and the actual area and write that as their 'score'. When they have completed the sheet, they total the scores. If they work competitively as a group in, the child with the smallest total wins.

Extension

Children could estimate then find the areas of the faces of objects in the classroom. They could also estimate larger areas in square metres.

Probing questions

- *What does 'area' mean?*
- *What tips would you give to someone trying to estimate the area of a rectangle?*
- *How would you estimate the area of this sheet?*

Checkpoints

- Does the child understand area measured in square centimetres?
- Can the child make a reasonable estimate of the area of a rectangle?
- Can the child use the formula for the area of a rectangle?

- Has difficulty in estimating areas
- Does not know or use the formula for finding the areas of rectangles

Watch for	Further experiences
Has difficulty in estimating areas	(1) Provide more experiences with transparent rectangles on a grid of centimetre squares.
Has poor understanding of area in terms of square centimetres/units	(2) Progress to opaque rectangles on a grid of centimetre squares; ask: *How many rows? How many squares in each row? So how many squares altogether?*
Does not know or use the formula for finding the areas of rectangles	(3) Move to rectangles without the grid. Let children measure the sides and work out the number of centimetre squares it covers.
Counts imaginary centimetre squares one by one	(4) Finally, they should be able to derive the formula for themselves in words.

CD links

See also *Can Do Maths* Year 5/P6 CD-ROM 3

Shape and space

Key objective

Recognise parallel and perpendicular lines, and properties of rectangles

Activity 1 Feeling shapes

Learning objective

Recognise parallel and perpendicular lines, and properties of rectangles

Organisation

Groups of three or four

Resources

A bag of shape tiles: regular and irregular shapes and different rectangles, including squares

Activity

Explain to the children that they are going to find out how good they are at identifying parallel and perpendicular sides in shapes and whether or not a shape is a rectangle. Give each group a bag of shapes tiles and let the children take turns to pick, but not withdraw, a shape from the bag. Ask them to feel the chosen shape and identify whether:

- the shape has right angles, and how many
- the shape has parallel sides, and how many pairs
- the shape is a rectangle (and if not, what shape it is).

The child takes the shape out of the bag and the group decides whether the identification was successful.

Probing questions

- *What makes you think that the shape is/is not a rectangle?*
- *What can you tell me about parallel/perpendicular lines?*
- *How would you check if two lines are parallel/perpendicular?*

Checkpoints

- Can the child identify parallel and perpendicular sides in shapes?
- Can the child identify the rectangles in a set of shapes?

- Has difficulty in recognising perpendicular lines unless they are in a horizontal/vertical orientation
- Has difficulty recognising parallel lines that are not the same length
- Is unclear about the properties of rectangles

Activity 2 Quadrilateral investigation

Learning objective

Recognise parallel and perpendicular lines, and properties of rectangles

Organisation

Individuals or groups of two or three

Resources

RS33 *Dotty grids*; 9-pin geoboards and elastic bands (not essential); coloured pencils

Activity

Give the children copies of RS33 *Dotty grids* and a geoboard and elastic bands. Ask the children to investigate the different quadrilaterals they can make on the geoboard, then record each one on RS33. You may wish to tell them that there are sixteen possibilities excluding reflections. They should indicate with coloured pencils or symbols any parallel and perpendicular lines in each shape. For example:

If geoboards are not available the children can work directly on to RS33.

Probing questions

- *How would you check if two lines are parallel/perpendicular?*

- *How can you know that this shape is/is not a rectangle?*
- *Is it possible for a quadrilateral to have exactly three right angles? Why?*

Checkpoints

- Can the child identify parallel and perpendicular lines in shapes, whatever the orientation?
- Can the child identify the rectangles in a set of shapes?

- Has difficulty in recognising perpendicular lines unless they are in a horizontal/vertical orientation
- Has difficulty in recognising parallel lines that are not the same length or are in an oblique orientation
- Is unclear about the properties of rectangles

Activity **3** Sorting quadrilaterals

Learning objective

Recognise parallel and perpendicular lines

Organisation

Groups of two or three

Resources

RS34 *Quadrilaterals*; RS35 *Sorting grid* enlarged to A3 size

Activity

Give each group a set of quadrilaterals cut out of RS34 *Quadrilaterals* and a copy of RS35 *Sorting grid*. Explain that they must put each quadrilateral in the correct space on the grid. If necessary demonstrate, with the children's help, what to do. Ensure that they understand that they must look for the number of *pairs* of parallel sides and count the right angles. Encourage the group to discuss and agree the results.

Extension

Children could draw quadrilaterals in the empty cells on the grid. Also, encourage them to write the names on any of the quadrilaterals they know.

Probing questions

- *Is it possible to have a quadrilateral with exactly three right angles? Why?*
- *How could you check that two lines are parallel/perpendicular?*
- *What is the same about an oblong and a square? What is different?*
- *Which of these shapes a rectangle? How do you know?*

Checkpoint

- Can the child recognise parallel and perpendicular lines in shapes, whatever the orientation?

- Has difficulty in recognising perpendicular lines unless they are in a horizontal/vertical orientation
- Has difficulty in recognising parallel lines that are not the same length or are in an oblique orientation

---

Watch for	Further experiences
Has difficulty in recognising perpendicular lines unless they are in a horizontal/vertical orientation	Explain that for lines to be perpendicular they must be at right angles. Give further practice in identifying perpendicular lines in oblique orientations, using a right angle measure to check. Identify perpendicular lines in the environment, for example in tile and fabric patterns.
Has difficulty in recognising parallel lines that are not the same length or are in an oblique orientation	Ensure that the children understand that the criteria for parallel lines is that they never meet (they are always the same distance apart). Provide more experiences of identifying parallel lines in a variety of orientations and of a variety of lengths and in the environment.
Is unclear about the properties of rectangles	Ensure that the children understand the main attributes of a rectangle. Give more experiences of identifying rectangles that are in unusual orientations and with unusual proportions such as long thin ones. Practise identifying rectangles in the environment.

CD links

See also *Can Do Maths* Year 5/P6 CD-ROM 3

Solving problems

Key objective

Use all four operations to solve simple word problems involving numbers and quantities, including time, explaining methods and reasoning

Activity 1 Time problems

Learning objectives

Use all four operations to solve simple word problems based on 'real life' involving time and explain methods and reasoning

Organisation

Individuals

Resources

RS36 *Time problems*

Activity

Give each child a copy of RS36 *Time problems*. Tell the children that there are five problems on different aspects of time to solve and that they must show how they solved each one in the space underneath. Explain that it is *how* they solve a problem and the strategies they use that are being assessed, as well as their ability to calculate correct answers. Point out that it is important that they show their workings and explain what they did in the space provided under each problem. Tell them that if they need more space they should use the back of the sheet.

Probing question

- *How did you solve this problem? Talk me through it step by step.*
- *How did you decide which part to do first?*
- *What tips would you give to someone about how to solve a problem?*

Checkpoints

- Does the child work in an organised way?
- Can the child choose and use appropriate number operations to solve problems?
- Can the child use appropriate ways of calculating?
- Can the child explain clearly how a problem was solved?

- Works in a disorganised way
- Has difficulty in choosing the appropriate operations
- Has a limited range of calculating strategies
- Has difficulty in explaining methods and reasoning

Activity 2 Practical problems

Learning objectives

Use all four operations to solve simple problems based on real life and explain methods and reasoning

Organisation

Individuals or groups of two or three

Resources

RS37 *Practical problems*; calculators; one or two 2p coins; a level surface; a medium-sized book; rulers

Activity

Give the children a copy of RS37 *Practical problems*, a calculator, some 2p coins, a book and a

ruler. Tell them that they should choose one of the two practical problems on the resource sheet. Explain that the purpose of the problems is to see how good they are at working out problem solving strategies rather than at calculating. Point out that they only need to put approximate answers and that they can use a calculator to do any calculations. It is important that they show in the space provided how they tackled each problem.

Probing question

- *How did you solve this problem? Talk me through it step by step.*
- *Is there another way you could have solved this problem?*

Checkpoints

- Does the child work in an organised way?
- Can the child use an efficient strategy?
- Can the child explain clearly their problem solving strategy?

- Works in a disorganised way
- Has difficulty in choosing the appropriate operations
- Has a limited range of calculating strategies
- Has difficulty in explaining methods and reasoning

| Activity | 3 | Mixed problems |

Learning objectives

Use all four operations to solve simple word problems involving numbers and quantities and explain methods and reasoning

Organisation

Individuals

Resources

RS38 *Mixed problems*

Activity

Give each child a copy of RS38 *Mixed problems* and tell them that it provides five problems involving numbers, money and measures. Explain that the first two problems can be solved in one step but the remaining three problems require two or more steps for their solution. Explain that it is *how* they solve a problem and the strategies they use that are being assessed, as well as their ability to calculate correct answers. Point out that it is important that they show their workings and explain what they did in the spaces provided. Tell them that if they need more space then they should use the back of the sheet.

Probing questions

- *How do you know whether to add, subtract, multiply or divide?*
- *How did you decide which part of the problem to do first?*
- *How did you solve this problem? Talk me through it step by step.*
- *What tips would you give to someone about how to go about solving a problem?*

Checkpoints

- Can the child work in an organised way?
- Can the child choose and use appropriate number operations to solve problems?
- Can the child use appropriate ways of calculating?
- Can the child explain clearly how a problem was solved?

- Works in a disorganised way
- Has difficulty in choosing the appropriate operations
- Has a limited range of calculating strategies
- Has difficulty in explaining methods and reasoning

Watch for	Further experiences
Works in a disorganised way	Provide practice with extremely simple multi-step problems with single-digit numbers so that the child can focus on strategy rather than the numbers and operations. Before they start on a problem ask them to list orally or in writing what they will do in order: *What will you do first? Then what will you do?*
Has difficulty in choosing the appropriate operations	Provide practice with problems involving very small numbers so that the child can focus on identifying the operations needed. When deciding which operation to use, encourage the children to ask questions such as *Will the answer be bigger or smaller?*
Has a limited range of calculating strategies	Over a period of time, increase the child's repertoire of mental and written calculating strategies.
Has difficulty in explaining methods and reasoning	Encourage children to explain to each other the methods they use to solve problems. Ask them to write, as if to a younger child, how they solved a problem. Encourage them to write what they did as a numbered list.

CD links

See also *Can Do Maths* Year 5/P6 CD-ROM 3

Matching calculations

Name --   **Date** --

Each calculation in one column has a partner with the same answer in the other column.
Join partners from dot to dot with straight lines.

12 × 10 •	A W	• 8000 ÷ 100
400 ÷ 10 •	K R	• 40 × 10
8 × 10 •	V E T	• 2400 ÷ 100
4000 ÷ 10 •	S L	• 1200 ÷ 10
600 ÷ 10 •	U L B	• 2400 ÷ 10
240 ÷ 10 •	A D	• 50 × 10
17 × 100 •	C O R	• 4000 ÷ 100
24 × 10 •	N	• 6000 ÷ 100
5 × 100 •	D O	• 2500 ÷ 10
25 × 10 •	E E	• 170 × 10

Some letters have a line going through them.
Write the letters in order from the top to bottom to find the hidden message.

___ ___ ___ ___ / ___ ___ ___ ___ !

Assess and Review Year 5/P6 © Paul Harrison, Nelson Thornes Ltd 2002

Real life problems

Name _____   **Date** _____

Answer these as quickly as you can.

1. 100 fans buy tickets for a pop concert.
   The tickets cost £15 each.
   How much do the fans pay altogether? _____

2. There are 2500 seats in a sports stadium.
   The seats are divided equally into 100 rows.
   How many seats are there in each row? _____

3. A box of 10 computer disks costs £6.
   How much does 1 computer disk cost? _____

4. A train starts off with 27 passengers.
   At the end of the journey there are
   10 times as many passengers.
   How many passengers is that? _____

5. A path is 25 metres long.
   How many centimetres is that? _____

6. Share £2500 equally between 10 people.
   How much do they each get? _____

7. John travels 100 miles each day.
   How far does John travel in 2 weeks? _____

8. How many 10 litre paint cans
   will 3500 litres of paint fill? _____

9. A wooden shelf is 60 centimetres long.
   How many metres of wood will be needed
   to make 100 shelves? _____

10. How many 10p coins are there in £295? _____

Dominoes 1

Copy the dominoes onto card and cut them out.

45	500 ÷ 10	50	37 × 100
3700	560 ÷ 10	56	35 × 10
350	500 ÷ 100	5	68 × 10
680	470 ÷ 10	47	78 × 100
7800	900 ÷ 100	9	79 × 10
790	550 ÷ 10	55	62 × 10

Dominoes 2

Copy the dominoes onto card and cut them out.

620	37 × 10

370	8320 ÷ 10

832	26 × 10

260	7700 ÷ 100

77	7 × 100

700	830 ÷ 10

83	780 ÷ 10

78	51 × 100

5100	5060 ÷ 10

506	64 × 10

640	26 × 100

2600	4500 ÷ 100

Ordering tracks

Cut out one track for each player.

✂- -

Name: _____

Name: _____

Name: _____

Name: _____

Name: _____

Copy and cut out the cards.

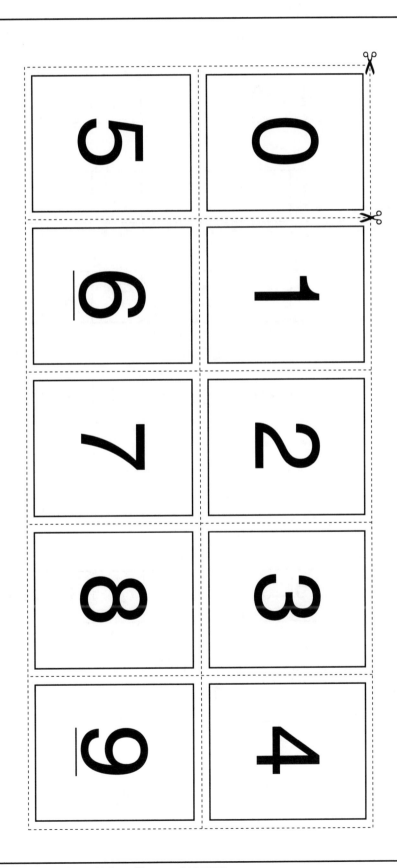

Negative–positive patterns

Name _____   **Date** _____

1

| −6 | | −4 | −3 | | | | 1 | | | |

2

| | | −3 | | | 0 | 1 | | | 4 | |

3

| | | | | −2 | 0 | 2 | 4 | 6 | | |

4

| −15 | | | −6 | | 0 | 3 | 6 | | 12 | |

5

| | | | | | −1 | 1 | 3 | | | |

6

| | | −12 | −8 | | | | 4 | 8 | 12 | |

7

| −20 | | | | 0 | 5 | | | | 25 | |

8

| | | | −10 | | | | 20 | 30 | | |

Temperature cards

Copy and cut out the cards.

−9 °C	−8 °C	−7 °C	−6 °C
−5 °C	−4 °C	−3 °C	−2 °C
−1 °C	0 °C	1 °C	2 °C
3 °C	4 °C	5 °C	6 °C
7 °C	8 °C	9 °C	10 °C

One-step targets

Name --

Date --

Write one operation in the circle that will change the start number to the target number.

Use a calculator to check.

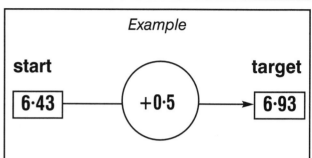

Example

start | target

6·43 → +0·5 → 6·93

1 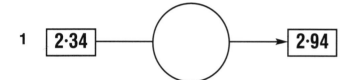 2·34 → ◯ → 2·94

2  4·75 → ◯ → 4·70

3  2·3 → ◯ → 23

4  14·25 → ◯ → 18·25

5  42 → ◯ → 4·2

6  36·34 → ◯ → 36·04

7 54·32 → ◯ → 54

8 14·83 → ◯ → 19·83

9  37·04 → ◯ → 37·94

10 235·10 → ◯ → 235·17

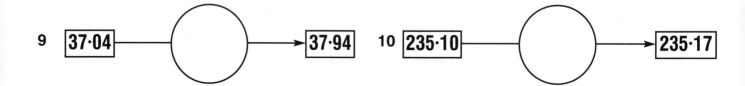

Rounding measures

Name ------------------------------------- **Date** -------------------------------------

1   Round each length in the table to the nearest metre.

Some of the longest snakes in the world

snake	length (m)	rounded length (m)
Royal python	10·7	
Diamond python	6·4	
King cobra	5·8	
Indian python	7·6	
Boa constrictor	4·9	
Bushmaster	3·7	
Giant brown	3·4	
Indigo	2·3	

2   Round each weight and length in the table to the nearest gram or centimetre.

Some of the smallest mammals in the world

mammal	weight (g)	rounded weight (g)	length (cm)	rounded length (cm)
pygmy shrew	1·5		3·6	
Kitti's hognosed bat	2·2		2·9	
pipistrelle bat	3·5		4·1	
masked shrew	2·3		4·6	
southern blossom bat	12·3		5·3	
little brown bat	7·9		3·8	
house mouse	12·4		6·4	
harvest mouse	4·7		5·7	

Rounding decimals

Name ---------------------------------- **Date** ----------------------------------

Round each decimal to the nearest whole number.

Write the decimal in one of the boxes next to its nearest whole number.

The first one is done for you.

| 35·2 | 43·5 | 39·5 | 41·7 | 36·9 | 42·4 | 37·8 |
| 39·14 | 38·95 | 43·50 | 37·34 | 36·32 | 43·44 | 41·32 |

	→ **35** ←	**35.2**
	→ **36** ←	
	→ **37** ←	
	→ **38** ←	
	→ **39** ←	
	→ **40** ←	
	→ **41** ←	
	→ **42** ←	
	→ **43** ←	
	→ **44** ←	

Now choose some numbers of your own to write in the spare boxes.

Calculator conversions

Name	Date
---	---

Complete these tables for converting fractions to decimals.
The first one has been done for you.

Make sure that you predict what each result will be before you use the calculator.

Table A

fraction	division	I think the result will be	calculator result
$\frac{1}{10}$	$1 \div 10$	0·1	0·1
$\frac{7}{10}$			
$\frac{9}{10}$			
$\frac{5}{100}$			
$\frac{16}{100}$			
$\frac{5}{10}$			
$\frac{50}{100}$			
$\frac{1}{2}$			
$\frac{25}{100}$			
$\frac{30}{100}$			

Table B

fraction	division	I think the result will be	calculator result
$\frac{1}{4}$			
$\frac{75}{100}$			
$\frac{3}{4}$			
$\frac{2}{10}$			
$\frac{4}{10}$			
$\frac{1}{5}$			
$\frac{2}{5}$			
$\frac{3}{5}$			
$\frac{4}{5}$			
$\frac{5}{5}$			

Finding fractions

Name -- **Date** --

Fractions of numbers

Write the answers.

1 $\frac{1}{4}$ of 16 = _____	4 $\frac{4}{5}$ of 20 = _____	7 $\frac{1}{3}$ of 21 = _____	9 $\frac{1}{100}$ of 500 = ____
2 $\frac{3}{4}$ of 16 = _____	5 $\frac{1}{10}$ of 30 = ____	8 $\frac{2}{3}$ of 21 = _____	10 $\frac{9}{100}$ of 500 = ____
3 $\frac{1}{5}$ of 20 = _____	6 $\frac{6}{10}$ of 30 = ____		

Fractions of lengths

Complete the tables.

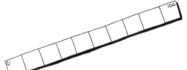

Table B

	number of centimetres
$\frac{1}{2}$ of 1 m	cm
$\frac{1}{4}$ of 1 m	cm
$\frac{3}{4}$ of 1 m	cm
$\frac{9}{10}$ of 1 cm	cm
$\frac{23}{100}$ of 1m	cm

Table A

	number of millimetres
$\frac{1}{2}$ of 1 cm	mm
$\frac{1}{4}$ of 1 cm	mm
$\frac{3}{4}$ of 1 cm	mm
$\frac{7}{10}$ of 1 cm	mm

Table C

	number of metres
$\frac{1}{2}$ of 1 km	m
$\frac{1}{4}$ of 1 km	m
$\frac{3}{4}$ of 1 km	m
$\frac{7}{10}$ of 1 km	m
$\frac{9}{100}$ of 1 km	m

Fraction cards

Copy and cut out the cards.

$\dfrac{1}{2}$	$\dfrac{1}{4}$	$\dfrac{2}{4}$	$\dfrac{3}{4}$
$\dfrac{1}{5}$	$\dfrac{2}{5}$	$\dfrac{3}{5}$	$\dfrac{4}{5}$
$\dfrac{3}{6}$	$\dfrac{2}{8}$	$\dfrac{4}{8}$	$\dfrac{1}{10}$
$\dfrac{2}{10}$	$\dfrac{3}{10}$	$\dfrac{4}{10}$	$\dfrac{5}{10}$
$\dfrac{6}{10}$	$\dfrac{7}{10}$	$\dfrac{8}{10}$	$\dfrac{9}{10}$
$\dfrac{1}{100}$	$\dfrac{10}{100}$	$\dfrac{25}{100}$	$\dfrac{75}{100}$

Decimal cards

Copy and cut out the cards.

0·5	0·25	0·5	0·75
0·2	0·4	0·6	0·8
0·5	0·25	0·5	0·1
0·2	0·3	0·4	0·5
0·6	0·7	0·8	0·9
0·01	0·1	0·25	0·75

Counting up

Name -- **Date** --

Find these differences by counting up.

Draw number lines to show the steps you took.

1 **207 − 75 = _____**

2 **108 − 76 = _____**

3 **308 − 269 = _____**

4 **3009 − 1095 = _____**

5 **2006 − 1420 = _____**

6 **3008 − 1478 = _____**

Multiple steps

Name	Date

Write what you need to add for each step.

Then work out the difference between the two numbers.

Example

346 ---- $\boxed{+54}$ ----➤ 400 ---- $\boxed{+22}$ ----➤ 422 $422 - 346 = \boxed{76}$

1   253 ---- $\boxed{+}$ ----➤ 300 ---- $\boxed{+}$ ----➤ 325 $325 - 253 = \boxed{}$

2   467 ---- $\boxed{+}$ ----➤ 500 ---- $\boxed{+}$ ----➤ 532 $532 - 467 = \boxed{}$

3   684 ---- $\boxed{+}$ ----➤ 700 ---- $\boxed{+}$ ----➤ 761 $761 - 684 = \boxed{}$

4   1993 ---- $\boxed{+}$ ----➤ 2000 ---- $\boxed{+}$ --➤ 2008 $2008 - 1993 = \boxed{}$

5   2975 ---- $\boxed{+}$ ----➤ 3000 ---- $\boxed{+}$ --➤ 3025 $3025 - 2975 = \boxed{}$

6   4750 ---- $\boxed{+}$ ----➤ 5000 ---- $\boxed{+}$ --➤ 5018 $5018 - 4750 = \boxed{}$

Column addition

Name -- **Date** --

587 + 475

Here are two column methods of doing this addition:

```
  587        587
+ 475      + 475
-----      -----
  900       1062
  150       1 1
   12
-----
 1062
```

Choose one of these methods or another method of column addition to do these. Estimate each answer first.

1 236 + 327
estimate =

2 425 + 291
estimate =

3 546 + 388
estimate =

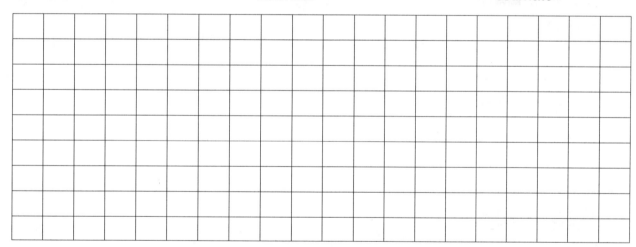

4 937 + 146
estimate =

5 3587 + 615
estimate =

6 2981 + 264
estimate =

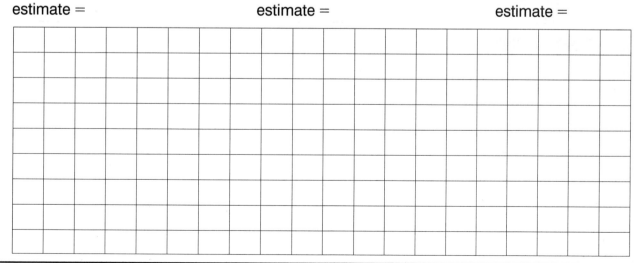

Column subtraction

Name -- **Date** --

---

754 − 236

Here are two methods of doing this subtraction:

$$754 = 700 + 50 + 4 = 700 + 40 + 14$$
$$-236 = 200 + 30 + 6 = 200 + 30 + 6$$
$$\overline{ 500 + 10 + 8} = 518$$

$$
\begin{array}{r}
{}^{4}{}^{1} \\
7\,\cancel{5}\,4 \\
-\,2\,3\,6 \\
\hline
5\,1\,8
\end{array}
$$

Choose one of the methods to do these. Estimate each answer first.

---

1 **534 − 225**

estimate =

---

2 **745 − 318**

estimate =

---

3 **623 − 155**

estimate =

---

4 **742 − 367**

estimate =

---

5 **848 − 271**

estimate =

Place the digits

Name	Date
-------------------------------------	-------------------------------------

Here are some digit cards.

4	4	5	5	6	6

Use the cards to make each addition or subtraction correct. You can use each card only once. You could use real digit cards to help you.

1

```
  ☐ ☐ ☐
+ ☐ ☐ ☐
-------
  9 1 2
```

2

```
  ☐ ☐ ☐
+ ☐ ☐ ☐
---------
1 0 1 1
```

3

```
  ☐ ☐ ☐
+ ☐ ☐ ☐
---------
1 2 0 0
```

4

```
  ☐ ☐ ☐
+ ☐ ☐ ☐
---------
1 0 2 9
```

5

```
  ☐ ☐ ☐
- ☐ ☐ ☐
-------
  2 0 9
```

6

```
  ☐ ☐ ☐
- ☐ ☐
-------
    9 9
```

Multiplication maze

Name .... Date ....

This activity will test how well you know the ×6, ×7, ×8 and ×9 tables.

Find a way through the maze. Follow the answers and collect the letters.
Write the letters in the boxes to find the hidden message.

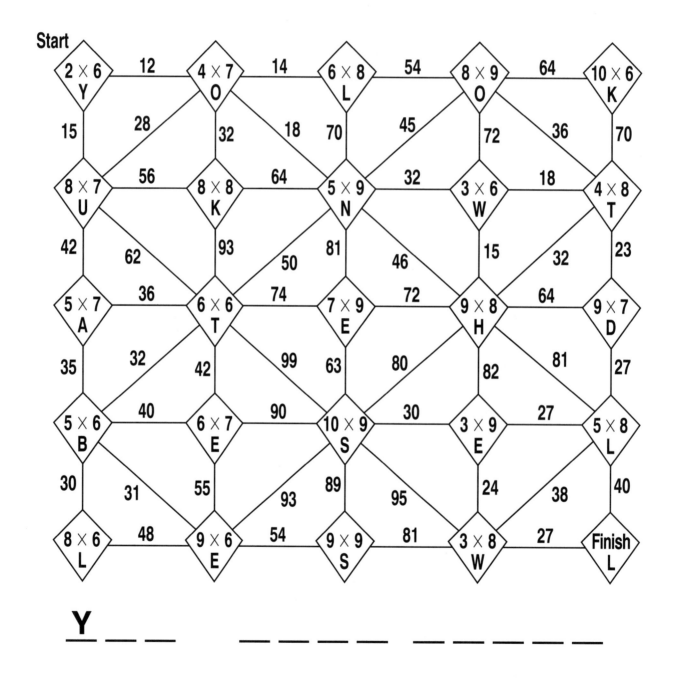

Y _ _   _ _ _ _ _ _ _ _ _

_ _ _ _ _ _ _ _ _ _

Speed tables

Name --- **Date** ---

Go down each ladder. Just write down the answers. Time yourself.

Try to do them all in less than five minutes.

Have a competition with some friends to see who is quickest.

1

2 × 4	
4 × 6	
7 × 4	
7 × 8	
5 × 4	
3 × 10	
7 × 7	
7 × 2	
8 × 5	
5 × 7	
5 × 10	
9 × 5	

2

4 × 3	
5 × 3	
5 × 9	
9 × 4	
8 × 9	
6 × 5	
4 × 9	
5 × 2	
3 × 8	
9 × 2	
6 × 3	
10 × 10	

3

3 × 9	
5 × 5	
2 × 10	
2 × 3	
6 × 6	
6 × 2	
7 × 6	
7 × 5	
8 × 10	
2 × 9	
10 × 3	
10 × 2	

4

8 × 4	
8 × 7	
9 × 6	
7 × 9	
9 × 8	
5 × 8	
9 × 7	
8 × 8	
9 × 10	
8 × 6	
4 × 7	
10 × 4	

I took [ ] minutes [ ] seconds.

Criss-cross tables

This is a game for two players.

You will need a calculator and counters in two colours.

Each choose a colour of counter.

Take turns to enter any multiplication from the ×2 to ×10 tables into the calculator.

If you see the answer below, put one of your counters on it.

The winner is the first with four counters in a line –
vertically, horizontally or diagonally.

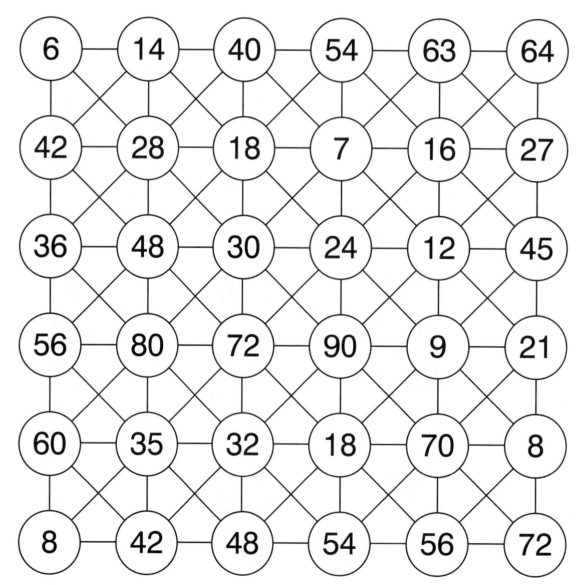

Board:

6	14	40	54	63	64
42	28	18	7	16	27
36	48	30	24	12	45
56	80	72	90	9	21
60	35	32	18	70	8
8	42	48	54	56	72

Multiple towers

This is a game for two or more players. You need two dice.

Each player has a grid. Write their names below.

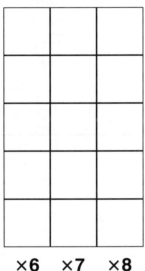

×6 ×7 ×8

_____

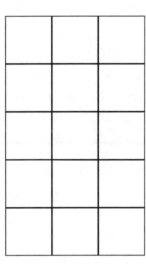

×6 ×7 ×8

_____

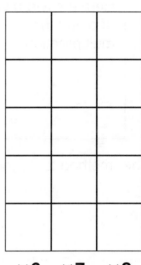

×6 ×7 ×8

_____

Take turns to roll the dice.

Use the results in any order to make a
2-digit number.

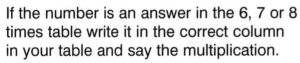

41 or 14

If the number is an answer in the 6, 7 or 8
times table write it in the correct column
in your table and say the multiplication.

If it is not, wait until your next turn.

You cannot have the same number more
than once in the same column.
But you can have the same number in
different columns.

The winner is the first to fill up all the columns.

**2 times 7
is 14**

14

×6 ×7 ×8

Short multiplication

Name ------------------------------------ **Date** ------------------------------------

---

346 × 9

Here are two methods
of doing this
multiplication:

$$
\begin{array}{r}
346 \\
\times \quad 9 \\
\hline
\end{array}
$$

$300 \times 9 \longrightarrow 2700$

$40 \times 9 \longrightarrow 360$

$6 \times 9 \longrightarrow 54$

$\overline{3114}$

$$
\begin{array}{r}
346 \\
\times \quad 9 \\
\hline
3114 \\
{}^{4\ 5}
\end{array}
$$

Choose either method to do these. Estimate each answer first.

1 236 × 3

estimate =

2 348 × 4

estimate =

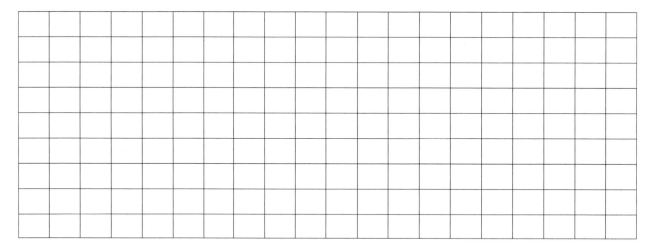

3 451 × 6

estimate =

4 237 × 9

estimate =

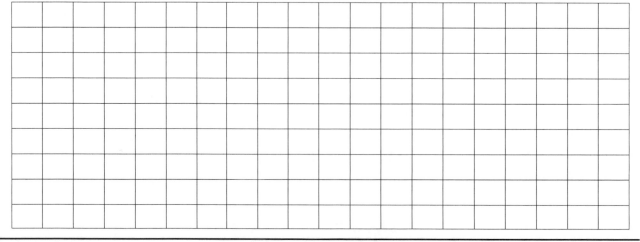

Short division

Name --

Date --

---

196 ÷ 6

Here are two methods
of doing this division:

```
   6)196
  - 180    30 × 6
    16
  -  12    2 × 6
     4
```

```
      32  R4
   6)196
     18
     16
     12
      4
```

Answer: 32 R4

Choose either method to do these. Estimate each answer first.

1   173 ÷ 4

estimate =

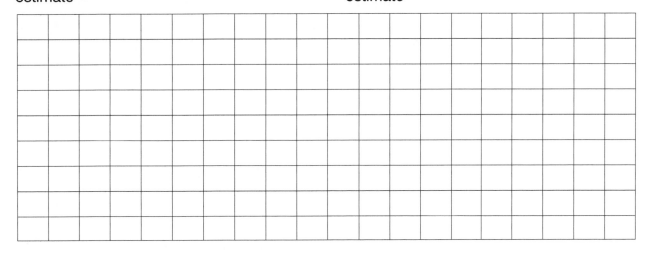

2   238 ÷ 5

estimate =

3   568 ÷ 6

estimate =

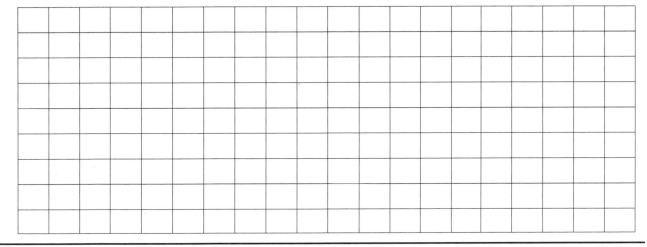

4   732 ÷ 8

estimate =

Long multiplication

Name ---

Date ---

Example:		72
72 × 38		× 38
	72 × 30 ⟶	2160
	72 × 8 ⟶	576
		2736
		1

Use the method in the example to do these. Estimate each answer first.

1 63 × 27

estimate =

2 54 × 39

estimate =

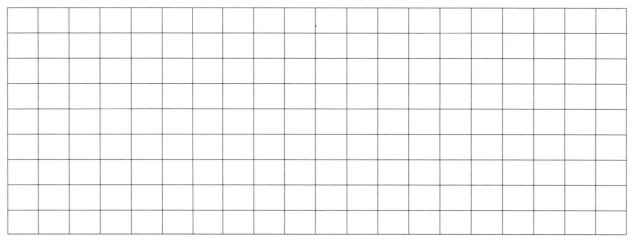

3 39 × 42

estimate =

4 78 × 35

estimate =

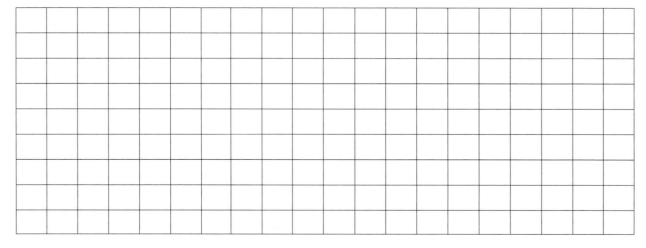

Comparing methods

Name	**Date**

Use the grid method to find the answer to these:

1 53 × 64

2 73 × 57

3 29 × 36

4 48 × 27

✂ -

Name	**Date**

Use the standard method of long multiplication to find the answer to these:

1			5	3				**2**			7	3					
	×		6	4					×		5	7					
3			2	9				**4**			4	8					
	×		3	6					×		2	7					

Areas of rectangles

Name -- **Date** --

Work out the area of each rectangle.

1 Area = _____ cm²

2 Area = _____ cm²

3 Area = _____ cm²

4 Area = _____ cm²

5 Area = _____ cm²

Grid of centimetre squares

Name -- **Date** --

Area problems

Name	Date

Solve these problems.

Show your working.

1   The cover of a book measures 10 cm by 8 cm. What is the area?

2   The area of one face of a cube is 6 cm². What is the total area of all the faces of the cube?

3   The area of a postcard is 150 cm². The width of the postcard is 10 cm. What is the length of the postcard?

4   A room measures 8 metres by 5 metres. What is the area of the room?

5   A gardener has 24 metres of fence. What is the biggest rectangular area of garden that she can enclose?

6   The perimeter of a square is 12 cm. What is the area of the square? [perimeter = distance all the way round]

Best estimator

Name	Date
--	---

Estimate the area of each picture. Then find out each area. The difference between your estimate and the actual area is your score. Aim for a low score!

1

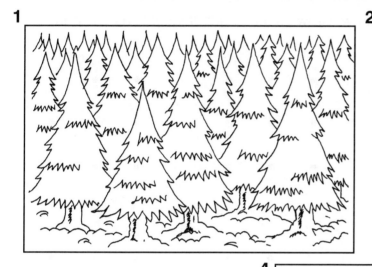

estimate _____

actual area _____

score _____

2

estimate _____

actual area _____

score _____

4

estimate _____

actual area _____

score _____

3

estimate _____

actual area _____

score

6

estimate _____

actual area _____

score

5

estimate _____

actual area _____

score

Dotty grids

Name -- **Date** --

Draw a different quadrilateral on each 3 × 3 grid. Each vertex must be on a dot.

Use coloured pencils or some other way to show right angles that are parallel.

Write the names of any quadrilaterals you know. Draw as many quadrilaterals as you can.

Quadrilaterals

Cut out the shapes.

Sorting grid

Name ------------------------------------- **Date** -------------------------------------

Number of pairs of parallel sides

Number of right angles	0	1	2
0			
1			
2			
3			
4			

Time problems

Name

Date

Solve these problems. Estimate each answer first.

Show your working underneath each problem.

1   A train leaves Astbury station at 10:45 and arrives at Bingley station at 15:46.
    How long does the journey last?

2   Today is January 23. My birthday is in exactly three weeks' time.
    What is the date of my birthday?

3   There are four laps in a relay race. Here are the times for each lap:
    lap 1: 76·7 seconds   **lap 2:** 82·1 seconds
    lap 3: 74·2 seconds   **lap 4:** 81·7 seconds.
    What was the total time for the four laps?

4   James records two programmes on a two-hour video tape.
    One programme is 35 minutes long. The other programme is 20 minutes long.
    How much time is there left on the tape?

5   A film lasts for 125 minutes. It starts at 7.15 p.m. What time does it end?

Practical problems

Name	Date

Choose one of these problems to solve. Show all your working and how you solved the problem. You can use a calculator.

Problem 1

Choose a small table or desk top. If you covered it with 2p coins, approximately how much would that be worth in pounds?

Problem 2

Pick a medium-sized book.

Work out approximately how many words it contains.

Approximately how many letters are there?

Mixed problems

Name	Date

Solve these problems. Estimate each answer first.

Show your working underneath each problem.

1   I have read 212 of the 500 pages in my book.
How many more pages must I read to finish the book?

2   There are 6 eggs in a box.
How many eggs are there in 12 boxes?
How many boxes will 120 eggs fill?

3   You buy 4 cans of cola. You give a £5 note.
You get £3 change. How much does 1 can of cola cost?

4   Jane has to take two 5 ml spoonfuls of medicine four times a day.
She has a 240 ml bottle of medicine.
How many days will the medicine last?

5   A television normally costs £300.
In a sale it is reduced by 25 %.
What is the sale price of the television?

Written assessment tests

Assessment tests

In this section there are two written tests and five mental mathematics tests. These tests can be used at any time after all of the key objectives for the year have been taught. They will be especially useful towards the end of the school year and will give evidence of achievement for the key objectives.

Written tests

There are two written tests to choose from. You may find it helpful, where children are sitting alongside each other, to use both tests, so that children will show their own work. Each test covers all of the thirteen key objectives for Year 5. No time limit has been set for the test. Either allow the children to work until they have completed all of the questions, or decide upon a time limit, such as 45 minutes.

After you have given out the answer sheets and before the children start the test:

- make sure that they have a pencil and ruler with centimetres; explain that using calculators is not allowed

- explain that in most cases answers are to be written in an answer box

- tell them that if they need to do any written working out they can do so anywhere other than in an answer box

- explain that in some cases there will be a larger box where they are actually asked to show their working; if they do not do this, they may not get any marks

- discourage the children from rubbing out; instead, they can put a line through an incorrect answer and put the second version alongside

- tell them how long they have to complete the test

- remind them that they must not talk during the test

- explain that if they find a question too difficult, they should move on to the next one and come back later if they have time.

During the test:

- informally monitor children's progress through the test and offer encouragement particularly to those experiencing any difficulties

- periodically tell the children how much time they have left.

If they finish the test early encourage them to go back and check their answers.

After the test is finished

Mark the answers. Where a child has made an error, refer back in this book to the relevant section for that key objective and use the probing questions and Watch for sections to help you determine what further help the child will need.

Written test key objectives

The table below shows the question numbers from Written assessment Tests 1 and 2 that correspond to each Year 5 key objective. Each key objective has also been given a letter of the alphabet, which is displayed in the margin of the test paper next to the corresponding question.

Key objectives	Test 1	Test 2
A Multiply and divide any positive integer up to 10 000 by 10 or 100 and understand the effect	1	1
B Order a given set of positive and negative integers	2	2
C Use decimal notation for tenths and hundredths	3	3
D Round a number with one or two decimal places to the nearest integer	4	4
E Relate fractions to division and to their decimal representation	5, 6	5, 6
F Calculate mentally a difference such as $8\,006 - 2\,993$	7	7
G Carry out column addition and subtraction of two integers less than 10 000	8	8
H Know by heart all multiplication facts up to 10×10	9	9
I Carry out short multiplication and division of a 3-digit by a single-digit integer	10	10
J Carry out long multiplication of a 2-digit by a 2-digit integer	11	11
K Understand area measured in square centimetres (cm^2); understand and use the formula in words 'length $\times$ breadth' for the area of a rectangle	13	12
L Recognise parallel and perpendicular lines, and properties of rectangles	14, 15	13, 14
M Use all four operations to solve simple word problems involving numbers and quantities, including time, explaining methods and reasoning	12	15

Test 1

Name .... **Date** ....

A ( ) 1

1 Write the digits of each answer in the correct boxes.

Tth	Th	H	T	U
		5	3	8

× 100

Tth	Th	H	T	U

Th	H	T	U
2	1	6	0

÷ 10

Th	H	T	U

B ( ) 1

2 Write these temperatures in order starting with the coldest.

    −8 °C   0 °C   4 °C   −5 °C   −1 °C   1 °C

C ( ) 1

3 Write what the digit 6 is worth in each number.

    3·06   6·03   36·3   3·63

D ( ) 1

4 Circle the number **nearest to 5**.

    5·09   4·98   5·1   5·25

E ( ) 1

5 Circle the decimal that is **equivalent to** $\frac{1}{4}$

    0·14   0·25   0·4   0·05

TOTAL

78

6 Match each box to the correct number.

One has been done for you.

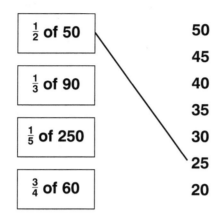

$\frac{1}{2}$ of 50	50
	45
$\frac{1}{3}$ of 90	40
	35
$\frac{1}{5}$ of 250	30
	25
$\frac{3}{4}$ of 60	20

E
1

7 Calculate the difference between 3975 and 7008 by **counting up**.

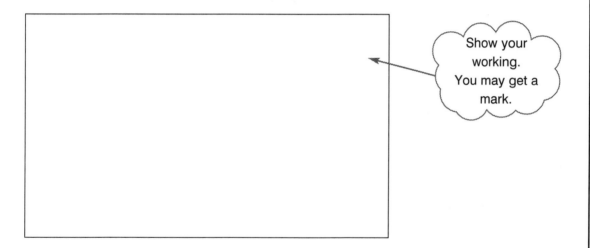

Show your working. You may get a mark.

F
2

8 Write the missing digits to make this correct.

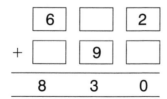

$$\begin{array}{ccc} 6 & \square & 2 \\ + \square & 9 & \square \\ \hline 8 & 3 & 0 \end{array}$$

G
1

9 Write the missing numbers.

$9 \times 9 = \boxed{}$ $6 \times \boxed{} = 54$ $\boxed{} \times 8 = 40$

H
1

TOTAL

79

I ◯
2

10 Calculate the answer.

$$639 \div 5 = \boxed{}$$

Show your working.
You may get a mark.

J ◯
1

11 Complete this long multiplication:

$$
\begin{array}{r}
3\,2 \\
\times\ 4\,8 \\
\hline
\end{array}
$$

M ◯
2

12 There are 532 children at Candale school.

219 children are boys.

How many are girls?

Show your working.
You may get a mark.

Assess and Review Year 5/P6 © Paul Harrison, Nelson Thornes Ltd 2002

13 What is the area of this picture?

Use a ruler.

Answer: [   ]

14 Circle the shape that is **not a rectangle**.

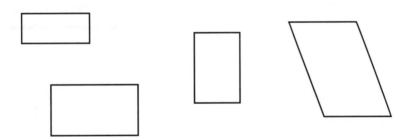

15 Circle the shape that has **exactly two pairs of parallel sides**.

Test 2

Name -- **Date** ---------------------------------

A 1

1 Write × 10, ÷ 10, × 100 *or* ÷ 100 in each box

64 ⬚ = 640   73 000 ⬚ = 730

B 1

2

| Temperature at 9.00 a.m. | Temperature at 1.00 p.m. |

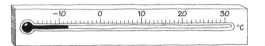 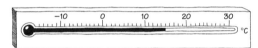

By how many degrees did the temperature rise between 9.00 am and 1.00pm? ⬚

C 1

3 Put these numbers in order starting with the **smallest**.

| 5·36 | 5·63 | 5·09 | 5·91 | 4·09 | 4·11 |

⬚ ⬚ ⬚ ⬚ ⬚ ⬚

D 1

4 Draw a line from each decimal to its nearest whole number.
One has been done for you.

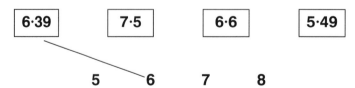

6·39   7·5   6·6   5·49

5   6   7   8

TOTAL

5 This table shows fractions and their decimal equivalents.

Complete the table.

Fraction	Decimal
$\frac{1}{4}$	
$\frac{1}{2}$	
$\frac{7}{10}$	
$\frac{3}{4}$	

6 Write how many pence.

$\frac{1}{4}$ **of £1 =** [ ] **p** $\frac{9}{10}$ **of £1 =** [ ] **p** $\frac{17}{100}$ **of £1 =** [ ] **p**

7 Calculate the difference between 1005 and 750 by **counting up**.

Show your working. You may get a mark.

8 Write the missing digits to make this correct.

5		2
−	5	
4	0	3

9 Write a number in each box to make the statement true.

6 × 6 = [ ] **× 4**   **5 × 8 =** [ ] **× 10**

I ◯ 2

10 Calculate the answer.

$$617 \times 8 = \boxed{}$$

Show your working. You may get a mark.

J ◯ 1

11 Is the answer to this long multiplication correct? Write yes or no.

$$
\begin{array}{r}
3\,6 \\
\times\ 2\,4 \\
\hline
7\,2\,0 \\
1\,5\,4 \\
\hline
8\,7\,4 \\
\end{array}
$$

36×20

36×4

$\boxed{}$

K ◯ 2

12 The area of a **square** photograph is 100 cm².

What is the **perimeter** of the photograph?

$\boxed{}$

Show your working. You may get a mark.

TOTAL

84

13 Write True or False for each statement.

a A rectangle has exactly **2 right angles**.

b The **opposite sides** of a rectangle are **perpendicular**.

c The **opposite sides** of a rectangle are **equal**.

d A rectangle has exactly **one pair of parallel sides**.

14 Put a cross (✗) on the two sides that are perpendicular.

15 A stamp album holds 235 stamps.

Liam has nine full albums, and one album with just 25 stamps.

How many stamps does he have altogether?

Show your working. You may get a mark.

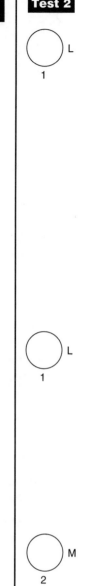

TOTAL

85

Mental mathematics tests

Mental mathematics tests

There are five general mental mathematics tests. Each test contains twenty questions. Five seconds are allowed for answering each of the first five questions; ten seconds for the next ten questions and fifteen seconds for the last five questions. Each test should take no longer than twenty minutes to administer. An answer sheet is provided for each test with aide-memoires for some of the questions.

Check that the children are sitting so that they can work individually. Provide each child with a pencil or pen and a copy of the answer sheet. Before the test begins, read out these instructions to the children:

- listen carefully to the instructions that I am going to give you; they will help you to complete the test

- check that you have an answer sheet and a pen or pencil *(pause)*

- you may not use an eraser, a calculator or any other mathematical equipment

- at the top of the paper write your name and the date *(pause)*

- there are twenty questions in the test

- work out the answers to the questions in your head before writing the answer

- there is an answer box for each question where you should write the answer to the questions and nothing else

- you may jot things down outside the answer box if it helps you

- if you write down a wrong answer, cross it out and write the new answer next to it

- try to answer as many questions as you can; if you cannot answer a question put a line in the box

- for some of the questions there is useful information on the sheet to help you, such as numbers used in the question

- I will read each question twice so you can hear it again

- there are three sets of questions; you will have five seconds to answer each question in the first set. This is five seconds: 1, 2, 3, 4, 5 *(count the seconds)*

- you will have ten seconds to answer each question in the second set

- you will have fifteen seconds to answer each question in the third set

- you may not ask any questions once the test has started so if you have any questions ask them now *(pause long enough to allow any questions to be asked)*.

After the test is finished

Mark the answers. Where a child has made an error, refer back in this book to the relevant section for that key objective and use the probing questions and Watch for sections to help you to determine what further help the child will need.

Mental test key objectives

The table below shows the questions numbers from Mental mathematics Tests 1 to 5 that correspond to each Year 5 key objective.

Key objectives	Test 1	Test 2	Test 3	Test 4	Test 5
A Multiply and divide any positive integer up to 10 000 by 10 or 100 and understand the effect	3, 5	3	1, 3, 5	7	5
B Order a given set of positive and negative integers					
C Use decimal notation for tenths and hundredths	13, 15, 19	4	18		4
D Round a number with one or two decimal places to the nearest integer		13		9	
E Relate fractions to division and to their decimal representations	4, 6, 14	6, 11, 20	4, 6, 14, 15	4, 6, 15 18	4, 6 15
F Calculate mentally a difference such as 8 006 − 2 993	8	8, 9	8, 19	8, 19	8
G Carry out column addition and subtraction of two positive integers less than 10 000					
H Know by heart all multiplication facts up to 10 × 10	2	2, 17	2	2, 3, 7	2, 3
I Carry out short multiplication and division of a 3-digit by a single-digit integer					
J Carry out long multiplication of a 2-digit by a 2-digit integer					
K Understand area measured in square centimetres (cm²); understand and use the formula in words 'length x breadth' for the area of a rectangle			11, 13, 20	11	
L Recognise parallel and perpendicular lines, and properties of rectangles		15		13	13
M Use all four operations to solve simple word problems involving numbers and quantities, including time, explaining methods and reasoning	7, 18, 20	7, 14, 18 19	7		7, 20

Mental mathematics test 1

You will have five seconds to work out each answer and write it down. *(Read each question twice and then allow five seconds before reading the next question.)*

1 How many twenty pence pieces are there in seven pounds?

2 Multiply nine by nine.

3 Divide four thousand three hundred by one hundred.

4 What is two-fifths as a decimal?

5 What is four hundred and thirty divided by ten?

For the next group of questions, you will have ten seconds to work out each answer and write it down. *(Read each question twice and allow ten seconds before reading the next question.)*

6 What is a third of six hundred and sixty?

7 My watch shows three forty-five a.m. What time was it fifty-five minutes ago?

8 What is one thousand and one subtract nine hundred and seventy-five?

9 What is the total of sixty-five, forty-nine and twenty-one?

10 What is double thirty-six point six?

11 The perimeter of a regular hexagon is one hundred and twenty-six centimetres. What is the length of one side?

12 What is twenty-five multiplied by thirty?

13 Look at your answer sheet. Put a ring around the biggest number.

14 One fifth of a number is thirteen. What is the number?

15 Look at your answer sheet. Put a ring around the decimal which is equivalent to ten hundredths.

For the next group of questions, you will have fifteen seconds to work out each answer and write it down. *(Read each question twice and allow fifteen seconds before reading the next question.)*

16 Add together fifteen, twenty-four and fifty-two.

17 Look at your answer sheet. Put a ring around the number that is a multiple of both five and three.

18 A gardener took four hours and twenty minutes to dig the borders of her garden. She finished at three o'clock. At what time did she start?

19 What number is half-way between three point five and thirteen point five?

20 Find the change from twenty-five pounds when you buy three shirts at six pounds fifty each.

That is the end of the test.

Put down your pencil or pen and have your answer sheet ready to be collected.

Mental mathematics

Test 1

Name		Date	

Time: five seconds for each question

1		20p £7

2		

3		4300

4		

5		430

Time: ten seconds for each question

6		660

7		3.45 a.m.

8		1001 975

9		65 49 21

TOTAL

10		36·6

11		126 cm

12		25 30

13	1·23 1·32 1·09 1·9 1·62

14	

15	0·01 0·1 1·0 0·2 0·5

Time: fifteen seconds for each question

16		15 24 52

17	53 35 105 155 76

18		4 hrs 20 mins 3 o'clock

19		3·5 13·5

20		£25 £6.50

Assess and Review Year 5/P6 © Paul Harrison, Nelson Thornes Ltd 2002

Mental mathematics test 2

You will have five seconds to work out each answer and write it down. *(Read each question twice and then allow five seconds before reading the next question.)*

1 How many fifty pence pieces are there in fifty pounds?

2 What is the product of eight and six?

3 Multiply five hundred and thirty by one hundred.

4 What is three-quarters as a decimal?

5 What is the total of twenty-one and nineteen?

For the next group of questions, you will have ten seconds to work out each answer and write it down. *(Read each question twice and allow ten seconds before reading the next question.)*

6 What is three-quarters of sixty?

7 How many minutes is it from six-thirty a.m to seven forty-five a.m?

8 What is the difference between five thousand and eight and four thousand nine hundred and seventy-five?

9 What must I add to thirty-six to get one hundred and twenty?

10 Double twenty-five point five then add twelve.

11 What is a half of two point six metres in centimetres?

12 What is four hundred and sixty divided by four?

13 Look at your answer sheet. Put a ring around the decimal that is nearest to five.

14 I spend three pounds twenty. I have one pound forty-five left. How much did I start with?

15 Look at your answer sheet. Put a ring around the lines that are perpendicular.

For the next group of questions, you will have fifteen seconds to work out each answer and write it down. *(Read each question twice and allow fifteen seconds before reading the next question.)*

16 Thirty-six add eighteen subtract twelve.

17 Look at your answer sheet. Put a ring around the number that is a square number and is a multiple of 4.

18 Ron buys an antique for eight hundred and eighty-seven pounds. He sells the antique for one thousand and twelve pounds. How much profit does he make?

19 In a sale a book has twenty-five per cent taken off the price. If the old price was twelve pounds forty what is the sale price?

20 One eighth of a number is two point five. What is the number?

That is the end of the test.

Put down your pencil or pen and have your answer sheet ready to be collected.

Mental mathematics

Test 2

Name	Date

Time: five seconds for each question

1		50p £50

2	

3		530

4	

5		21 19

Time: ten seconds for each question

6		60

7	minutes	6.30 a.m. 7.45 a.m.

8		5008 4975

9		36 120

10		25·5 12

TOTAL

92

| 11 | cm | 2·6 m |

| 12 | | 460 |

| 13 | 4·09   4·91   5·02   5·2 |

| 14 | | £3·20   £1·45 |

| 15 | 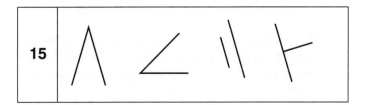 |

Time: fifteen seconds for each question

| 16 | | 36   18   12 |

| 17 | 64   25   49   24 |

| 18 | | £887   £1012 |

| 19 | | £12·40 |

| 20 | | 2·5 |

TOTAL

Mental mathematics test 3

You will have five seconds to work out each answer and write it down. *(Read each question twice and then allow five seconds before reading the next question.)*

1 How many ten pence pieces are there in four pounds?

2 Multiply six by eight.

3 Divide four hundred and eighty by ten.

4 What is one-quarter as a decimal?

5 What is four thousand two hundred divided by one hundred?

For the next group of questions, you will have ten seconds to work out each answer and write it down. *(Read each question twice and allow ten seconds before reading the next question.)*

6 What is a half of six hundred and eighty?

7 My watch shows two-forty a.m. What time will it show in thirty-five minutes?

8 What is one hundred subtract thirty-six?

9 What is two hundred and forty-five centimetres rounded to the nearest metre?

10 What is double twenty-five point five?

11 The length of a rectangle is nine centimetres. The width is six centimetres. What is the area of the rectangle?

12 What is nine multiplied by twenty-five?

13 Look at your answer sheet. Put a ring around the parallel lines.

14 One third of a number is twenty-five. What is the number?

15 Look at your answer sheet. Put a ring around the decimal which is equivalent to three-fifths.

For the next group of questions, you will have fifteen seconds to work out each answer and write it down. *(Read each question twice and allow fifteen seconds before reading the next question.)*

16 Add together fifteen, twenty-four and fifty-two.

17 Look at your answer sheet. Put a ring around the number that is a multiple of twenty-five.

18 Look at your answer sheet. Put a ring around the biggest number.

19 What is the difference between five thousand and four and three thousand nine hundred and ninety-seven?

20 The area of a square is 25 square centimetres. What is the perimeter of the square?

That is the end of the test.

Put down your pencil or pen and have your answer sheet ready to be collected.

Mental mathematics

Test 3

Name	Date

Time: five seconds for each question

1		10p £4

2	

3		480

4	

5		4200

Time: ten seconds for each question

6		680

7		2.40 a.m.

8	

9		245 cm

TOTAL

10		25·5

95

11	cm²	9 cm 6 cm

12		9 25

13	/\ \\ | L

14	

15	0·03 0·5 0·6 0·35 0·3

Time: fifteen seconds for each question

16		15 24 52

17	55 240 150 310 520

18	0·38 0·83 3·38 3·08 3·8

19		5004 3997

20		25 cm²

Mental mathematics test 4

You will have five seconds to work out each answer and write it down. *(Read each question twice and then allow five seconds before reading the next question.)*

1 How many fifty pence pieces are there in four pounds?

2 Multiply seven by six.

3 Divide seventy-two by nine.

4 What is three quarters as a decimal?

5 What is one point two five multiplied by four?

For the next group of questions, you will have ten seconds to work out each answer and write it down. *(Read each question twice and allow ten seconds before reading the next question.)*

6 What is a quarter of four hundred and eighty?

7 How many minutes are there in three hours?

8 What is two hundred subtract one hundred and seventy-two?

9 What is one kilogram six hundred and twenty-five grams rounded to the nearest kilogram?

10 What is double sixteen point five?

11 The area of a square is one hundred square centimetres. What is the length of one side of the square?

12 What is seventy-five multiplied by three?

13 Look at your answer sheet. Put a ring around the perpendicular lines.

14 Five times a number is one hundred and twenty-five. What is the number?

15 Look at your answer sheet. Put a ring around the decimal which is equivalent to two fifths.

For the next group of questions, you will have fifteen seconds to work out each answer and write it down. *(Read each question twice and allow fifteen seconds before reading the next question.)*

16 Add together twelve, forty-two and thirty-two.

17 Look at your answer sheet. Put a ring around the number that is divisible by four.

18 Look at your answer sheet. Put a ring around the smallest number.

19 What is the difference between three thousand and four and one thousand seven hundred and fifty?

20 Look at your answer sheet. Put a ring around the shape that has exactly two lines of symmetry.

That is the end of the test.

Put down your pencil or pen and have your answer sheet ready to be collected.

Mental mathematics

Test 4

Name		Date	

Time: five seconds for each question

1		50p £4

2	

3		72

4	

5		1·25

Time: ten seconds for each question

6		480

7	

8	

9	kg	1 kg 625 g

TOTAL

10		16·5

98

Assess and Review Year 5/P6 © Paul Harrison, Nelson Thornes Ltd 2002

11	cm	100 cm²

12		75 3

13	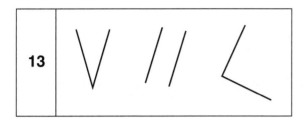

14		125

15	0·02 0·25 0·5 0·2 0·4

Time: fifteen seconds for each question

16		12 42 32

17	232 498 122 134

18	0·27 0·72 0·07 0·7 0·2

19		3004 1750

20	

Assess and Review Year 5/P6 © Paul Harrison, Nelson Thornes Ltd 2002

TOTAL

Mental mathematics test 5

You will have five seconds to work out each answer and write it down. *(Read each question twice and then allow five seconds before reading the next question.)*

1 How many twenty pence pieces are there in two pounds?

2 Multiply nine by eight.

3 Divide fifty-six by eight.

4 What is fifty-seven hundredths as a decimal?

5 What is fifty-eight multiplied by one hundred?

For the next group of questions, you will have ten seconds to work out each answer and write it down. *(Read each question twice and allow ten seconds before reading the next question.)*

6 What is half of one hundred and sixty?

7 The time is thirteen forty-five. What time will it be in twenty minutes?

8 What is the difference between thirty-eight and one hundred?

9 What is four hundred and twenty centimetres to the nearest metre?

10 What is double thirteen point five?

11 Each side of a hexagon is eleven centimetres. What is the perimeter of the hexagon?

12 What is eleven multiplied by twelve?

13 Look at your answer sheet. Put a ring around the perpendicular lines.

14 What is the remainder when you divide one hundred and seven by three?

15 Look at your answer sheet. Put a ring around the decimal which is equivalent to four fifths.

For the next group of questions, you will have fifteen seconds to work out each answer and write it down. *(Read each question twice and allow fifteen seconds before reading the next question.)*

16 Add together thirty-nine, forty and forty-one.

17 Look at your answer sheet. Put a ring around the number which is a multiple of both three and five.

18 Look at your answer sheet. Put a ring around the biggest number.

19 Calculate eleven minus one point three.

20 The price of a television is two hundred pounds. In a sale the price is reduced by ten per cent. What is the sale price of the television?

That is the end of the test.

Put down your pencil or pen and have your answer sheet ready to be collected.

Mental mathematics

Test 5

Name	Date

Time: five seconds for each question

1		20p £2

2	

3		56

4	

5		58

Time: ten seconds for each question

6		160

7		13:45

8	

9		420 cm

10		13·5

TOTAL

11		11 cm

12		11 12

13	

14		107 3

15	0·04 0·45 0·4 0·8 0·5

Time: fifteen seconds for each question

16		39 40 41

17	35 53 150 250

18	0·19 0·01 0·09 0·1 0·2

19		11 1·3

20		£200 10%

TOTAL

102

Answers

Resource sheets

RS1 Matching calculations
WELL DONE

RS2 Real life problems

1	£1500	6	£250
2	25	7	1400 miles
3	60p	8	350
4	270	9	60 metres
5	2500 cm	10	2950

RS7 Negative-positive patterns

1 −6 −5 −4 −3 −2 −1 0 1 2 3 4
2 −5 −4 −3 −2 −1 0 1 2 3 4
3 −10 −8 −6 −4 0 −2 0 2 4 6 8
4 −15 −12 −9 −6 −3 0 3 6 9 12
5 −9 −7 −5 −3 −1 1 3 5 7 9
6 −20 −16 −12 −8 −4 0 4 8 12 16
7 −20 −15 −10 −5 0 5 10 15 20 25
8 −40 −30 −20 −10 0 10 20 30 40 50

RS9 One-step targets

1	+ 0·6	6	+ 0·3
2	− 0·05	7	− 0·32
3	× 10	8	+ 5
4	+ 4	9	+ 0·9
5	÷ 10	10	+ 0·07

RS10 Rounding measures

1

Some of the longest snakes in the world

snake	length (m)	rounded length (m)
Royal python	10·7	11
Diamond python	6·4	6
King cobra	5·8	6
Indian python	7·6	8
Boa constrictor	4·9	5
Bushmaster	3·7	4
Giant brown	3·4	3
Indigo	2·3	2

2

Some of the smallest mammals in the world

mammal	weight (g)	rounded weight (g)	length (cm)	rounded length (cm)
pygmy shrew	1·5	2	3·6	4
Kitti's hognosed bat	2·2	2	2·9	3
pipistrelle bat	3·5	4	4·1	4
masked shrew	2·3	2	4·6	5
southern blossom bat	12·3	12	5·3	5
little brown bat	7·9	8	3·8	4
house mouse	12·4	12	6·4	6
harvest mouse	4·7	5	5·7	6

RS11 Rounding decimals

Decimals for each rounded number can be in either column. Check that the child's own numbers for the remaining boxes round to the number in the centre column.

☐	→ 35 ←	35·2
36·32	→ 36 ←	☐
36·9	→ 37 ←	37·34
37·8	→ 38 ←	☐
39·14	→ 39 ←	38·95
39·5	→ 40 ←	☐
41·32	→ 41 ←	☐
41·7	→ 42 ←	42·4
43·44	→ 43 ←	☐
43·5	→ 44 ←	43·50

RS12 Calculator conversions

Table A

fraction	division	I think the result will be	calculator result
$\frac{1}{10}$	1 ÷ 10	0·1	0·1
$\frac{7}{10}$	7 ÷ 10	Answers will vary	0·7
$\frac{9}{10}$	9 ÷ 10		0·9
$\frac{5}{100}$	5 ÷ 100		0·05
$\frac{16}{100}$	16 ÷ 100		0·16
$\frac{5}{10}$	5 ÷ 10		0·5
$\frac{50}{100}$	50 ÷ 100		0·5
$\frac{1}{2}$	1 ÷ 2		0·5
$\frac{25}{100}$	25 ÷ 100		0·25
$\frac{30}{100}$	30 ÷ 100		0·3

Table B

fraction	division	I think the result will be	calculator result
$\frac{1}{4}$	$1 \div 4$	0·1	0·25
$\frac{75}{100}$	$75 \div 100$	Answers will vary	0·75
$\frac{3}{4}$	$3 \div 4$		0·75
$\frac{2}{10}$	$2 \div 10$		0·2
$\frac{4}{10}$	$4 \div 10$		0·4
$\frac{1}{5}$	$1 \div 5$		0·2
$\frac{2}{5}$	$2 \div 5$		0·4
$\frac{3}{5}$	$3 \div 5$		0·6
$\frac{4}{5}$	$4 \div 5$		0·8
$\frac{5}{5}$	$5 \div 5$		1

RS13 Finding fractions

1 4
2 12
3 4
4 16
5 3
6 18
7 7
8 14
9 5
10 45

Table A

	number of millimetres
$\frac{1}{2}$ of 1 cm	5 mm
$\frac{1}{4}$ of 1 cm	2·5 mm
$\frac{3}{4}$ of 1 cm	7·5 mm
$\frac{7}{10}$ of 1 cm	7 mm

Table B

	number of centimetres
$\frac{1}{2}$ of 1 m	50 cm
$\frac{1}{4}$ of 1 m	25 cm
$\frac{3}{4}$ of 1 m	75 cm
$\frac{9}{10}$ of 1 cm	90 cm
$\frac{23}{100}$ of 1m	23 cm

Table C

	number of metres
$\frac{1}{2}$ of 1 km	500 m
$\frac{1}{4}$ of 1 km	250 m
$\frac{3}{4}$ of 1 km	750 m
$\frac{7}{10}$ of 1 km	700 m
$\frac{9}{100}$ of 1 km	900 m

RS16 Counting up

1 132
2 32
3 39
4 1 914
5 586
6 1 530

Steps will vary. Check that they are efficient and include steps to multiples of 10, 100 or 1 000.

RS17 Multiple steps

1 253 --- +47 --➤ 300 --- +25 --➤ 325   325 − 253 = 72
2 467 --- +33 --➤ 500 --- +32 --➤ 532   532 − 467 = 65
3 684 --- +16 --➤ 700 --- +61 --➤ 761   761 − 684 = 77
4 1993 -- +7 --➤ 2000 --- +8 --➤ 2008 2008 − 1993 = 15
5 2975 -- +25 --➤ 3000 --- +25 --➤ 3025 3025 − 2975 = 50
6 4750 -- +250 --➤ 5000 --- +18 --➤ 5018 5018 − 4750 = 268

RS18 Column addition

1 563
2 716
3 934
4 1 083
5 4 202
6 3 245

RS19 Column subtraction

1 309
2 427
3 468
4 375
5 577

RS20 Place the digits

In the additions, digits in columns may be reversed.

1	4 5 6	3	5 5 6	5	6 5 5
	+ 4 5 6		+ 6 4 4		− 4 4 6
2	4 6 6	4	5 6 5	6	5 6 4
	+ 5 4 5		+ 4 6 4		− 4 6 5

RS21 Multiplication maze

YOU KNOW THESE TABLES WELL

RS22 Speed tables

1 8 24 28 56 20 30 49 14 40 35 50 45
2 12 15 45 36 72 30 36 10 24 18 18 100
3 27 25 20 6 36 12 42 35 80 18 30 20
4 32 56 54 63 72 40 63 64 90 48 28 40

RS25 Short multiplication

1 708   2 1 392   3 2 706   4 2 133

RS26 Short division

1 43 R 1   2 47 R 3   3 94 R 4   4 91 R 4

RS27 Long multiplication

1 1 701 **2** 2 106 **3** 1 638 **4** 2 730

RS28 Comparing methods

1 3 392
2 4 161
3 1 044
4 1 296

RS29 Areas of rectangles

1 12 cm²
2 27 cm²
3 25 cm²
4 64 cm²
5 42 cm²

RS31 Area problems

1 80 cm²
2 36 cm²
3 15 cm
4 40 m²
5 36 m²
6 9 cm²

RS32 Best estimator

1 54 cm²
2 32 cm²
3 35 cm²
4 20 cm²
5 18 cm²
6 6 cm²
Estimates and scores will vary.

RS33 Dotty grids

square   square   rectangle   square

trapezium   trapezium   parallelogram

 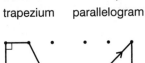

arrowhead   kite   trapezium

 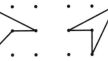

parallelogram   arrowhead

RS35 Sorting grid

Number of right angles	Number of pairs of parallel sides		
	0	**1**	**2**
0	Irregular quadrilateral, Kite	Isosceles trapezium	Rhombus, Parallelogram
1	Check children's own quadrilateral	Impossible quadrilateral	Impossible quadrilateral
2	Check children's own quadrilateral	Right-angled trapezium	Impossible quadrilateral
3	Impossible quadrilateral	Impossible quadrilateral	Impossible quadrilateral
4	Impossible quadrilateral	Impossible quadrilateral	Square, Rectangle

RS36 Time problems

1 5 hours 1 minute
2 February 13
3 314·7 seconds or 5 minutes 14·7 seconds
4 1 hour 5 minutes
5 9.20 p.m.

RS37 Practical problems

Answers will vary. Check the children's strategies and workings.

RS38 Mixed problems

1 288   **2** 72; 20   **3** 50p   **4** 6 days   **5** £225

Written test 1

1

Tth	Th	H	T	U		Tth	Th	H	T	U
		5	3	8	× 100		5	3	8	0	0

Th	H	T	U		Th	H	T	U
2	1	6	0	÷ 10		2	1	6

2 −8 °C −5 °C −1 °C 0 °C 1 °C 4 °C

3 6 hundredths ($\frac{6}{100}$) 6 units (ones) 6 units (ones)
6 tenths ($\frac{6}{10}$)

4 4·98 should be circled

5 0·25 should be circled

6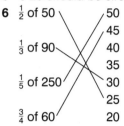
$\frac{1}{2}$ of 50 — 50
— 45
$\frac{1}{3}$ of 90 — 40
— 35
$\frac{1}{5}$ of 250 — 30
— 25
$\frac{3}{4}$ of 60 — 20

7 3 033 Allow an extra mark for clear correct working.

8   6 3 2
     + 1 9 8
     ———
      8 3 0

9 81 9 5

10 127 R 4 Allow an extra mark for clear correct working.

11   3 2
       × 4 8
      ———
     1 2 8 0
       2 5 6
      ———
     1 5 3 6

12 313 Allow an extra mark for clear correct working.

13 21 cm^2

14 The parallelogram should be circled.

15 The parallelogram should be circled.

Written test 2

1 ×10 ÷100

2 23 °C

3 4·09 4·11 5·09 5·36 5·63 5·91

4   6·39   7·5   6·6   5·49

    5   6   7   8

5

Fraction	Decimal
$\frac{1}{4}$	0·25
$\frac{1}{2}$	0·5
$\frac{7}{10}$	0·7
$\frac{3}{4}$	0·75

6 25p 90p 17p

7 255 Allow an extra mark for clear correct working.

8   5 6 2
     − 1 5 9
     ———
      4 0 3

9 9 4

10 4936 Allow an extra mark for clear correct working.

11 No

12 40 cm Allow an extra mark for clear correct working.

13 a False b False c True d False

14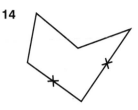

15 2 140 Allow an extra mark for clear correct working.

Mental mathematics test 1

1 35
2 81
3 43
4 0·4
5 43
6 220
7 2.50 a.m.
8 26
9 135
10 73·2
11 21 cm
12 750
13 1·9
14 65
15 0·1
16 91
17 105
18 10:40
19 8·5
20 £5.50

Mental mathematics test 2

1 100
2 48
3 53 000
4 0·75
5 40
6 45
7 75 minutes
8 33
9 84
10 63
11 130 cm
12 115
13 5·02
14 £4.65
15
16 42
17 64
18 £125
19 £9.30
20 20

Mental mathematics test 3

1   40
2   48
3   48
4   0·25
5   42
6   340
7   3.15 a.m.
8   64
9   2 metres
10 51
11 54 cm²
12 225
13

14 75
15 0·6
16 91
17 150
18 3·8
19 1 007
20 20 cm

Mental mathematics test 4

1   8
2   42
3   8
4   0·75
5   5
6   120
7   180
8   28
9   2 kg
10 33
11 10 cm

12 225
13

14 25
15 0·4
16 86
17 232
18 0·07
19 1 254
20 The rectangle should be circled.

Mental mathematics test 5

1   10
2   72
3   7
4   0·57
5   5 800
6   80
7   14:05
8   62
9   4 m
10 27
11 66 cm
12 132
13

14 2
15 0·8
16 120
17 150
18 0·2
19 9·7
20 £180